"THOSE
PECULIAR
AMERICANS"

Books by Lawrence H. Fuchs

POLITICAL BEHAVIOR OF
AMERICAN JEWS

HAWAII PONO: A SOCIAL HISTORY

JOHN F. KENNEDY AND AMERICAN
CATHOLICISM

"THOSE PECULIAR AMERICANS"

The Peace Corps and

LAWRENCE H. FUCHS

Professor of American Civilization and Politics
Brandeis University

MEREDITH PRESS : NEW YORK

"THOSE PECULIAR AMERICANS"

American National Character

To Janet Pearl, Frances Sarah, and Naomi Ruth,
who, in their own way, were pioneers
in the Peace Corps, too.

Acknowledgments

: I began work on this book during the summer of 1964 when I was Visiting Fellow at the Western Behavioral Sciences Institute in La Jolla, California, where conditions were ideal for writing.

During the academic year that followed, work on the manuscript came to a virtual standstill due to other professional and civic obligations; but during the academic year 1965–1966, I was given a sabbatical leave by Brandeis University which I spent as a Senior Scholar at the East-West Center at the University of Hawaii. As was true at WBSI, I again gained freedom to write in a congenial, stimulating and humanistic atmosphere.

During this time, I have had excellent secretarial assistance from Mrs. Jean Haskell in Waltham, Miss Kay Falbo at

WBSI, Miss Lorraine Tani and Miss Barbara Duke at the East-West Center, and Miss Linda Giardina at Brandeis University.

Of the several ex-Peace Corps volunteers and Filipinos who read the manuscript in the summer of 1966, I especially want to thank Mike Foreman and Jim Stewart for their helpful criticisms and suggestions.

My largest debt, of course, is to the volunteers whose emotions, ideas, and words are communicated through me in the pages to follow.

Foreword

> These Americans are an unusual people. When they see a problem—a canal to be dug or a school to be built—they immediately form a group or committee, whatever is necessary to get the job done.
>
> —Tocqueville, *Democracy in America*

: In his great book, Tocqueville described the developing American character and style by contrasting what he observed and sensed with what he knew from his own French experience; it is from this latter perspective that the American ability to form voluntary associations appears unusual. Professor Fuchs reverses this procedure and asks what is peculiar about Americans by contrast with the Filipinos, not so much in Manila but in the towns and villages where Peace Corps volunteers came as teacher aides under his supervision. He was the go-between, making arrangements on the one side with educational authorities in the Philippines, and on the other with the Peace Corps in Washington, the State Department and AID representatives on the scene, and the often anxious, hypercritical, and vulnerable volunteers in the field. If the latter had, as Dr. Fuchs describes it, a "non-job," taxing by its very amorphousness, he was overemployed to the point of exhaustion by trying conscientiously to respond to all the conflicting pressures and misunderstandings. This book, recollected in relative tranquility, is an effort to understand better the character of the volunteers as Americans, by seeing where were the sticking-points in their efforts to ingratiate, to integrate, and also to accomplish something in the Philippines.

Many of the volunteers, and other like-minded Americans I have seen preparing to go overseas, have been thoroughly imbued with the doctrine of cultural relativity; they share the happy belief that all peoples are at bottom really human and that with goodwill and sympathy they can communicate with each other. (They may sometimes fail to take elementary precautions of health or safety in their desire to share the lot of the poor they are going to help; and in fact, one apparent finding of some Peace Corps research is that the greater the physical hardships of groups of volunteers, the higher their morale—in part because the hardships are a solace against the ambiguities of the work itself.) Whether to the slums of our cities or to peasant cultures elsewhere, these mostly young and well-educated Americans come with a certain humility and not with the cultural arrogance and superciliousness of many previous generations of conquerors, traders, missionaries, and diplomats.

All the more, then, the discovery that there is something American about them surprises. It is not that they had expected to go native. But they had thought, many of them, that they were alienated from most of their fellow-Americans, by their lack of greed for status, their hostility to American chauvinism or rampant materialism, and their will-

ingness to treat as persons host-country nationals lacking in
the usual appurtenances of powerful weapons, stalled traffic,
the handsomeness of the well-to-do, and the other amenities
of abundance. In fact, among Filipino reactions that most
offended them was the nearly omnipresent desire for all
those American assets that they regarded as superficial and
cheap: Coca-Cola and light skin-color, movie Westerns and
big cars, popular music (not folk-rock) and big-time sports.
In these matters, like many other peoples, Filipinos wanted
to become Americanized. George M. Guthrie, Professor of
Psychology at Pennsylvania State University, who helped
train some of the volunteers in Dr. Fuchs's care, writes as
follows:

> The unfailing hospitality and deference of the Filipinos,
> coupled with the facts that many of them can express them-
> selves in English and show understanding of some Western
> values, often lead the American to feel at ease and to assume
> that he can function much as he would in the United States.[1]

Since this cultural similarity is superficial, the American
may be thrown off-balance when a situation revealing the
enormous disparity arises. According to Dr. Fuchs, the
volunteers soon discovered the tight networks of obligation
(*utang na loob*) on which Filipinos depend and which provide security while limiting individualism. They also dis-

---

[1]*See George M. Guthrie, "Cultural Preparations for the Philippines,"
in Robert B. Textor, ed.,* Cultural Frontiers of the Peace Corps, *Cambridge, Mass., M.I.T. Press, 1966, p. 24. This volume includes an excellent essay by David L. Szanton, "Cultural Confrontation in the
Philippines," describing some of the experiences of one of the early
volunteers; the other essays, whether by volunteers or by academicians
such as Textor himself, belong on the small shelf of books that can
moderate but never completely obviate "culture shock" for Americans
planning to work in unprotected settings outside of "PX country" overseas. Indeed, since the Philippines are in a sense an ex-colony, some of
the British novels of colonialism might be useful preliminary reading
also; I think of George Orwell's* Burmese Days *and* Shooting an Ele-
phant, *and the great African novels of Joyce Cary, and of Forster's*
Passage to India. *So too Elenore Smith Bowen's anthropological and
only semi-fictional account,* Return to Laughter, *conveys some of the
emotional miseries of cross-cultural encounter.*

covered *pakikisama,* a corollary emphasis on endlessly
smoothed personal relations that ruled out the candor and
directness the young Americans particularly valued. Cor-
respondingly, efforts at accomplishment in and out of the
schoolroom were met with a frustrating compound of friendliness, sabotage, delay, and what the volunteers regarded as
insincerity. The volunteers could have accepted straightfor-
ward resistance, but were depressed and baffled by repeated
promises that were then not fulfilled. (They may have
lacked a sufficient sense of the extent to which all poor peoples, including our own deprived Negroes and rural poor
whites, have been the recipients of promises in which they
dared not believe.) Sooner or later, the volunteers grew impatient with fatalism, with nepotism, with nonascetic priests
(a special problem for the many Catholic volunteers), and
with the double standard which chained women and gave
men free license.

The egalitarianism of the volunteers is perhaps the most
revolutionary, if impalpable, value that they bring. Dr.
Fuchs quotes a discerning volunteer who felt that in the
classroom he had left behind "a silent campaign against the
tryranny of the powerful."

Yet many of the more introspective volunteers were not
certain of the value even of such a legacy. As their own
previously submerged values were called into question by
their encounters, and as they continued to oppose the more
obvious forms of cultural imperialism, they wondered what
right they had to try to change another culture—even one
that insisted that it wanted change. When they discovered
that they could influence their Filipino counterparts by
manipulating *utang na loob* and saturating themselves in
pakikisama, they worried both about the compromises that
they were making with their own standards of integrity and
candor and about the imposition from above of their own
values and aims in spite of their egalitarianism. These are
much the same problems that have haunted many sensitive
whites working in the civil rights movement with bashful or

less-educated Negroes, or in urban poverty programs such as those of SDS. According to Dr. Fuchs, some of the volunteers appear to have concluded that it was all right to manipulate the Filipino social network provided that they themselves were changed by their exposure to it.

And indeed many were changed. Dr. Fuchs pictures the volunteers as very much in the American grain of atomistic and even touchy individualism, which he characterizes by reference to Emerson's precepts, writing: "Emerson's way of defending his own extreme shyness in relationships with others was to elevate the qualities of self-sufficiency and separateness to moral virtues and to seek refuge in nature." The volunteers would return to America with a greater appreciation for personalism, even for the social networks that bound people in; they would return less driven, accustomed to life on a different timetable and to the pleasantness (as Florence Kluckhohn might phrase it) of being valued for "being" rather than "doing."

Dr. Fuchs writes as if all this were quite novel and as if the volunteers had gone overseas with an unmitigated drive for achievement and a relatively flat and undifferentiated relationship to others. But while he labels his book as one about national character, it is not psychoanalytically oriented and does not treat the volunteers as individuals; it stays rather on the level of values, ideals, and patterns that are certainly widely shared among Americans, but in my judgment not universally shared. When he speaks of the loneliness and emptiness of human relations in America, which volunteers discovered when involved in *pakikisama,* I thought of the many volunteers I have known who entered the Peace Corps precisely because they were already aware of this emptiness and who came from sophisticated backgrounds, devaluing achievement and so exalting friendship that hardly any relations could meet their expectations. To be sure, for volunteers from a more provincial background, this discovery of the emptiness of their previous relations with people would come as a revelation. When I talked with the volunteers in Bogota about to return to the United States, I felt that the experience for them had depended very much on what they had been to begin with. For example, the political activists who had worked during their college years on behalf of civil rights or peace had sometimes become less dogmatic, less sure of the value or even of the possibility of social change. Sometimes they no longer believed that a few villainous elites kept the world poor and warlike—even in Colombia. At the same time their experiences had made them more compassionate toward the follies and errors of their own country, which appeared less vicious and detestable in cross-cultural perspective. In contrast, those many volunteers who had come from less cosmopolitan backgrounds were returning to the United States with an unquestioning commitment on the race question, in part the product of their emotionally intense and even searing involvement with a darker people of Indian or Mestizo blood. In this group, some who were Catholic had been shocked by the lack of dedication and even corruption of many Colombian village priests, and had had the bad luck not to encounter anyone like the late Father Camilo Torres, or the other exemplars of the new wave of social consciousness in the worker-priest mode; their faith had sometimes been shaken, or at any rate they had been led to re-examination. If some of the activists had been slowed down, these other volunteers had as it were been speeded up. In all this, Dr. Fuchs would emphasize what they shared as Americans, and indeed volunteers of both types found solace as well as frustration in a culture not dominated by the Protestant ethic and where personal relations counted for more than productivity. They would return less sure of their own cultural values, although much more aware of them.

If differences among volunteers affect, as they obviously do, the nature of their overseas experience, it is also obvious that the nature of the host country affects that experience. I believe that those engaged in Latin America and elsewhere in community development face problems comparable to those of the Philippine non-teacher in his non-job, while some who are teaching secondary school in Africa may be tied into a going concern in an almost patriarchal way. The frustrations of volunteers coming up against the greater apathy and poverty of some rural villages in India are perhaps even greater than those recounted in this book, perhaps the more so because of the British overlay, at least in the official strata. Indeed I think one could make an excellent study of American character types by a more systematic effort to examine this variety of cross-cultural encounters, each an unstandardized Rorschach to bring out the quintessentially American.

In this respect, Dr. Fuchs's emphasis on the near-solipsistic individualism of Americans seems right to me. Many of the volunteers I have seen, whether for the Peace Corps or Accion in Venezuela or for other such groups, value their own independence and autonomy in an almost anarchic way. The psychiatrist Dr. Robert J. Lifton, in his study of similar phenomena, speaks of the fear of "counterfeit nurturance" among people for whom even genuine nurturance may appear a threat. In the Peace Corps these attitudes lead volunteers to what seems to the outsider an almost paranoid, prickly, and unforgiving attitude toward headquarters, whether in Manila or Washington—a combination of insistence on support and resistance even to mild regulation comparable to the attitudes toward parents, teachers, and other adults. And of course the fact that for most of the volunteers in the Philippines this was their first experience in a bureaucracy, in a complex work setting, means that the Peace Corps suffered from the working out of anti-authority feelings and for its inevitable failure to live up either to the high ideals of its own most charismatic leaders or to the "image" which developed back home of the Noble American, which none of the volunteers can abide, haunted as they are by the ambiguity of their own motives and the all too evident inadequacy of their own performance.

The volunteers were so idealized at home, Dr. Fuchs suggests, partly because of the impact of *The Ugly American,* a book whose emphasis on the rugged pastoral virtues is in my judgment clouded by its rampant nationalism. Despite its anti-imperialist outlook, the Peace Corps remains an American agency, whereas in a happier world it would be an international one, drawing recruits from many different cultures, both in training and in the field.[2]

Everywhere in the less developed world people say that what they want is Western technology and Eastern (or African, or Latin American) values. This is a book that among other things raises the question as to whether such syncretism is possible. The volunteers found themselves caught up on just this point. They were in effect being asked to bring progress to the villages (in education, in housing, in hygiene, in agriculture, and so on) but to do so in terms acceptable or at least not intrusive vis-à-vis the Filipinos and their values. They were thus being required to meet two cultural payrolls at the same time; as Dr. Fuchs shows in vivid detail, the price for this was enormous frustration, self-deprecation, and scapegoating. All reform of a culture from without, including the sub-cultures of the deprived in our own society, raises similar questions. If the reformers are sensitve and nonexploitative, they face moral problems that earlier generations of colonizers mostly dodged. Most of these volunteers could not simply "Enjoy, enjoy"—they were too conscientious, if you like, too "American," for that, however hedonistic they might seem in contrast, let us say, to Swiss or Germans.

Many people hope, Dr. Fuchs and this writer among them, that the Peace Corps may have its principal effect upon the United States, as better prepared volunteers return in larger numbers, first to secure (as nearly half now do)

[2] *Leading Peace Corps officials are themselves similarly persuaded. They have sought to encourage the formation of comparable voluntary services in other countries, and have sponsored an exchange Peace Corps to the United States; but at least as long as the war in Vietnam goes on, to go further than this toward a wholly international agency seems politically unfeasible.*

further academic training and then to enter programs coping with the underdevelopment of our own society. One
major such underdevelopment is our residual yet tenacious
ethnocentrism, even among the educated; and many returned volunteers do regard this as on their agenda, both vis-
à-vis the country where they served and other countries in
general. *"Those Peculiar Americans"* helps place this issue
in cross-cultural perspective, offering vicarious exposure to
the majority, while reminding the tiny but growing minorities who have served overseas of what they were up against
as Americans.

DAVID RIESMAN

Brattleboro, Vermont
December 26, 1966

Contents

"THOSE
PECULIAR
AMERICANS"

Introduction

: As I bounded out of the Pan American clipper onto the concrete landing apron at the old Manila International Airport shortly after 8 A.M. on September 1, 1961, a score of Filipino photographers and newspapermen greeted me with popping flashbulbs and sharp questions. "What do you hope to accomplish in the Philippines?" "Will Americans be able to live in the barrios?" "Don't you think we need money and equipment, not Peace Corps volunteers?" "What can you tell us about the Peace Corps?"

What could I tell them! In five weeks, 128 volunteers would report for action in the Philippines, assigned to remote villages to perform as "educational aides," a title and concept completely new to Filipinos, volunteers, and myself. I told the reporters it was too early to answer their questions, but

3

of one thing I was certain. We *americanos* expected to learn more than we would teach. I never dreamed just how complex and painful a learning experience most volunteers actually would have.

It was a profound learning experience for me, too. No one really had any idea what the job of a Peace Corps Representative would be. For me, it was a time of testing, of learning about my strengths and weaknesses, as I never had before. Beyond knowledge gained about myself, the Peace Corps taught me more about American values and character and American government and politics than I had learned in ten years of teaching American Civilization and Politics at Harvard and Brandeis universities. It also taught me something about problems in human communication, particularly across cultures, and vastly changed my understanding of the problems of developing nations and the definition of development itself.

When John F. Kennedy was elected President, I was Dean of Faculty at Brandeis University in Waltham, Massachusetts. As a senator, Kennedy had read several of my articles and a book written by me. I had written a speech for him and followed his quest for the Presidency with high hopes that he would apply his forceful, fresh, and innovative mind to break the stalemate of the cold war and to promote human decency, economic prosperity, and political stability in the developing countries of Asia, Africa, and Latin America. There was no question in my mind that I would leave my university post at the end of the academic year for some position in the new administration. In the months following his election, it became clear that Kennedy's inaugural plea to ask not what your country could do for you but what you could do for your country in promoting peace and human freedom had been given singular expression in the creation of the Peace Corps.

A friend of mine, Harris Wofford, then serving as the President's assistant on civil rights and Peace Corps, introduced me to R. Sargent Shriver, Kennedy's brother-in-law and

Peace Corps Director, immediately after the Brandeis June commencement. Shriver and I talked about the indivisibility of the human community, the need for Americans to recapture their revolutionary fervor, and the desperate gap in material welfare between the rich and poor nations. Shriver was imbued with a missionary zeal to advance human understanding everywhere in the world. I welcomed his idealism because I also believed, and emphatically still do, that participation in the Peace Corps presents an extraordinary opportunity, not only for personal enrichment and growth, but for the promotion of world community. Shriver asked me to direct a program in the Philippines, which was to be the largest by far and in many ways the most difficult, and I was sworn in as Director in July.

A year later Shriver made his first overseas inspection trip. At that time approximately one third of all Peace Corps volunteers overseas were assigned in the Philippines. As we flew over the island of Panay, headed south from Manila to the central Visayan Islands to see volunteers in their communities and schools, Shriver turned to me and abruptly asked: "Hey, Fuchs, why don't you write a book about the Peace Corps when you go back to being a professor?"

Shriver's question—like a left jab from a boxer—may have been a feint, a decoy. He may have been thinking, Does this guy plan to go back to teaching college? What use can I make of him next year? Or it could have been a straight probe for information going out of his insatiable curiosity about almost anyone and anything.

"No, I don't think I'll write a book about the Peace Corps," I said in reply. "Why not?" he shot back another query.

The conversation about the book did not last longer than five minutes, but I remember it vividly because I had given Shriver's question serious thought before he asked it and turned it over in my mind many times afterward.

At that moment I was thoroughly involved in my administrative responsibilities in the Philippines, where I was in charge of what was to become the largest American government nonmilitary overseas field operation in history. I was interested only in supporting my staff and more than three hundred volunteers in the field and in preparing for the more than three hundred soon to come. We lived from crisis to crisis, and there was no time to keep a diary or even take notes, let alone do systematic research. Dozens of volunteers were shaken and depressed by the experience of trying to work in a strange culture. A boy for whom I had developed a deep affection had died of an amoebic abscess of the liver only a short time before. What mattered to me at the moment was the success of the volunteers, not an interpretation of them.

Now, in writing this book, I want to interpret the Peace Corps volunteers and their story just as clearly and sensitively as I am able. There are three reasons. The first results from conversations with ex-volunteers who speak and write of their inability to communicate the richness and complexity of their Peace Corps experience to those who have not shared it. They feel the Peace Corps and the volunteers are still not understood in the United States; and they are unhappy over what appears to them to be superficial or glib interpretations of their experience.

The second reason for writing this book stems from my growing desire to understand American values and character. It seems axiomatic to me that effectiveness in communication, especially across cultures, depends in large measure on our ability to assess our own values and motivations as Americans—to understand the Americanness aspects of ourselves. One of the best ways to do this is to study the behavior of Americans overseas, particularly those who live and work in another culture.

Finally, and to me most importantly, I am convinced that by trying to understand the complex story of Peace Corps volunteers, many of us will become better human beings. That is because most Peace Corps volunteers actually do become much better human beings after two years in the Peace Corps. As I read their experience, they become better for two reasons. The first is that they are given the chance to cast off facades and defenses in their relationships with others. They are not in a position of having to fight siblings or parents—only substitutes and themselves—or competing for grades or bucking for a promotion or a raise. They have the time and encouragement to learn how to be more truly themselves and how to listen more deeply and sensitively to others. They practice both and grow in the process.

Almost as important, it seems to me, is that they practice in relationships outside their own culture. Volunteers are forced to confront the narrowness not just of their special individuality but of their special culture, and they develop large insights into themselves and life because of it. To be more open and honest with oneself and others in a sensitive, caring way is a good beginning to becoming a better person, and to do that in another culture by surmounting the anxiety and fatigue of the encounter is to enlarge substantially one's intellectual and emotional capacities.

Now, before you begin the book, a reminder that it is about Americans. It is about Filipinos, too, but mainly as they are perceived by Americans. Filipinos are pictured with perceptual distortions that stem from the biases of our own culture. Americans usually don't see Filipinos the same way they see themselves, although I believe that many Peace Corps volunteers became increasingly empathic in their relationships to Filipinos. I ask the reader, particularly the Filipino reader, who, having gone through chapters 2, 3, and 4, is tempted to put down this book with a sense of dismay at the partial view of Filipino life presented through the words of Peace Corps volunteers, to continue on to chapters 5 and 6. It is not that I claim to have captured in words and understanding the full flavor and complexity of Filipino life. It is that, while the early chapters take the volunteers through their periods of shock and fatigue, through their deepest disappointments and negative feelings, the latter pages bring them, through their struggles, to a time of decreased defensiveness toward and more sensitive awareness of Filipinos.

I run the risk in these earlier pages of hurting Filipinos who may be stunned at the harsh and sometimes distorted reactions of Peace Corps volunteers to their culture. I ask them to read on in order to see how we *americanos* grew in our appreciation and love for Filipinos—my love for and joy with Filipino friends is extremely important to me—and also to see more clearly that this book is primarily about the limitations and potentialities of Americans, not Filipinos. For this book could have been written about the Peace Corps volunteers in at least a dozen other countries.

Volunteers in the Philippines who thought they were reacting to "Filipinoness" were many times responding to attitudes and behavior which were not specifically Filipino but which are common to Asia or even generic to traditional or poorer countries. Wherever Peace Corps volunteers have gone, eventually they have seen that their extraordinary emphasis on personal independence and achievement makes them peculiar. But at first it seems to them that the Afghans, Colombians, Micronesians, Nigerians, Turks, Thais, and Filipinos are the strange ones.

Where resources are scarce and traditions pervasive, it is not personal independence or achievement which is valued but mutual dependency and harmony within the in-group (family, tribe, or clan) and protection of that group against outsiders. Many actions stemming from those values and ascribed to Filipino culture could also be found in immigrant subcultures in the United States as well as on the continents of Asia, South America, and Africa.

Peace Corps volunteers who have served in other countries or Vista volunteers who have worked on Indian reservations or in urban ghettos will recognize in Filipinos many of the same values and attitudes which they found in their hosts and friends from the "other-culture." They will be struck particularly by the relative absence of achievement motivation and the high degree of personalization of Filipino life.

Those qualities usually are present where people are terribly poor and see no way of becoming richer, whether they live in a culture where traditions are powerful, as in Thailand, or in the Negro ghettos of our big cities.

So in large measure the Filipino setting in this book is interchangeable with other settings, because the cultural baggage that middle-class American Peace Corps volunteers carry and their reactions to and their ways of coping with the other-culture are the same in all the countries in which they live. None of this is to say that there are not special qualities that go into the making of a Filipino culture and a Filipino national character. It is to emphasize again that this is a book about Americans and their struggle to be more human in relationships with Filipinos who share much more with the rest of the world than they do with us. Like the vast majority of the world's peoples, Filipinos are traditional, poor, rural, darker-skinned, and not Protestant. It is we Americans, because of our extraordinarily peculiar history and inheritance, who are different.

When I left the Philippines in June, 1963, more than five hundred of the 630 volunteers on assignment were educational aides in the public schools. A group of about forty volunteers worked in the central high schools as teachers and coteachers of science. Approximately thirty worked in the normal schools and universities as utility teachers. And a group of twenty-two volunteers assisted Filipino barrio community development workers on the island of Mindanao. The elementary school program dwarfed the others, and to a considerable extent was seen by Filipinos and Americans as the Peace Corps in the Philippines; and it is mainly the story of the volunteers who served as educational aides that is told in the pages to come.

What follows is the story of the first of America's Peace Corps volunteers in the Philippines and my interpretation of what that story means, especially to Americans. It is told mainly from my memory and from the hundreds of passionately honest letters and reports written to me by volunteers who learned to care deeply about the ultimate questions of human life and death, and to experience the pains and satisfactions that come with service in the Peace Corps.

I
Ask not ...

: To a considerable extent, the Peace Corps was born out of America's historic sense of mission to protect liberty at home and spread it abroad. By liberty, Americans usually have meant personal independence—the right and capacity to make choices in selecting mates, jobs, domiciles, religions, and rulers. The European social philosophers of the eighteenth century had given (or seemed to give) primacy to the individual; but Americans took the Enlightenment faith in the individual and carried it to greater extremes than any people in history. The American cult of the individual has no parallel because its sources are unique to American history.

INDEPENDENCE AND ACHIEVEMENT: THE PROTESTANT SOURCE

North America was settled by Protestant dissenters who not only inherited the Reformation tradition which attacked the centrality of papal and hierarchical authority in the Church, but who dissented even from the Protestant Church of England. The central Protestant notion of a priesthood of all believers, each capable of experiencing God directly, interpreting that experience, and giving witness to it provided a ready basis to subvert authority not only in the Church but also in government and even in families. Those Protestant principles, planted on a moving frontier in a land of relatively abundant resources where labor was in short supply and which was open to immigrants from lower classes all over the world, helped promote the cult of individualism which foreigners have seen as distinctively American ever since the eighteenth century.

Most writers on the influence of Protestantism have followed Max Weber, whose thesis *The Protestant Ethic and the Spirit of Capitalism* emphasized the impetus which the Protestant Reformation gave to the development of Western capitalism by insisting that work was a worthwhile activity in its own right, that economic judgments be made on rational grounds without regard to tradition, and by disdaining personal indulgence. Luther's concept of a calling for every man has been stressed, as has Calvin's emphasis on predestination and the psychological need of men to demonstrate their salvation visibly through worldly success. But, in my view, the significance of Protestantism as it relates to the development of an American ideology is that it stressed individual effort in the quest for salvation, not simply that it sanctified economic entrepreneurship, which is merely one way of demonstrating one's worth.

Protestantism has not been a religion to worship nature, honor ancestors, or unite a historic community. It has been a religion to save, discover, and fulfill the self. In the seventeenth century this most often meant the salvation of souls.

It meant being touched by God's grace and bearing witness to one's renewal. Later it usually meant self-sufficiency in the race up the ladder of success and achievement. More recently it has begun to mean the actualization of the psychological self or the discovery and fulfillment of one's deepest nature. The Protestantism of Cotton Mather insisted upon a decision for Christ; the Protestantism of William McKinley glorified the achieving man; post-Freudian Protestantism stresses knowing and being true to one's inner self. In three hundred years the emphasis has shifted from religious to physical to emotional athleticism, but the moral injunction for the individual to assert his selfhood, independent of others and free from the restraints of tradition and authority, remains strong.

OPEN AND ABUNDANT LAND

The ideal of personal independence inherent in the central Protestant concept of salvation directly through experience with God was nourished by the sparsely settled, well-endowed land of America. The rigid subordination of factions, classes, or even of women and children in families (as intended by Puritan leaders) could not long be maintained where land and water were readily available and labor in short supply. The physical conditions of America put a premium on the qualities which later came to be associated with success on the frontier, the qualities of the pioneer (a concept and a word which has no analogue in any Filipino dialect). The frontier was peopled mainly by farmers whose ownership of land meant that each man and his family could work for themselves and enjoy a moral and economic independence unknown in Europe. It was the thesis of historian Frederick Jackson Turner that individualism was born under such conditions. The wilderness, he said, produced a kind of primitive organization based on the family where, "the tendency is anti-social. It produces antipathy to control, and particularly to any direct control." The frontier breaks the bonds of custom "and unrestraint is triumphant." In his article on the Middle West, Turner described the traits of the pioneer as "individual activity, inventiveness and competition." The Middle Western man "honored the man whose eye was quickest and whose grasp was the strongest in this contest." It was "every man for himself." It was in "the atomic conditions of the backwoods society that the individual was exalted and given free play . . . he fashioned a formula for social regeneration—the freedom of the individual to seek his own." The frontier fostered individualism, and highly individualistic Americans sought the frontier, and the nineteenth-century legends of pioneers and western heroes such as Buffalo Bill Cody, Daniel Boone, John C. Frémont, and Kit Carson stir the American imagination to this day with images of totally self-reliant and independent men.

There was disease and sometimes the savage opposition of Indians on the frontier, and infant mortality was extremely high, but there was an abundance in the earth which made individualism possible. Even in New England, where the land was hard, water was plentiful and a variety of crops could be produced. Elsewhere nature was more generous. There was usually an abundance of fowl, timber, fruits, and minerals. Stephen Vincent Benét has imagined the natural wealth which impressed the eyes of Virginia's first settlers in his poem *Western Star:* [1]

> Squash-vine and pumpkin-seed and the deer's sinew
> And the yellow, life-giving corn. . . .
> The fish that had never struck at an iron hook,
> The beaver, breeding faster than men could kill, . . .
> It was the first flood of Virginia Spring,
> White with new dogwood, smelling of wild strawberries,
> Warm and soft-voiced, cornflower-skied and kind.
> And they were ravished with it, after the sea, . . .

[1] Western Star *by Stephen Vincent Benét. Published by Holt, Rinehart & Winston. Copyright 1943 by Rosemary Carr Benét. Reprinted by permission of Brandt & Brandt.*

Oh, the fair meadows, the goodly trees and tall,
The fresh streams running in silver through the woods!
'Twas a land, a land!

The earth yielded to hard work and gave promise of more
to come, tempting men to hope for themselves and even
more for their children. In 1797, immediately following a
series of bloody Indian fights, a Kentuckian looked at his soil
"so rich, a clime so pure," where "plenty spreads her gen'rous
board" and "poverty must stay behind." Beyond Virginia
and Kentucky were the prairies, the Great Plains, and the
cornucopia of wealth of the Far West. In such a land men
and women did not have to protect their lives through a
tightly organized system of hierarchical authoritarian relationships. Individualism was a luxury which relatively
abundant resources made possible. In this milieu children
were encouraged to be independent, wives were called upon
to be partners rather than subordinates, and established authority in the church, government, or through elites of any
kind were challenged ritualistically. Long after the frontier
was officially closed, and even where there was a scarcity of
land and natural resources as in the islands of Hawaii, immigrants from Europe and Asia (even those from non-Protes-
tant backgrounds) discovered that abundance in America
cut the ties of hierarchy and authority within families and
encouraged the assertiveness of even women and children.

THE IMMIGRANT SOURCE

Although immigrant fathers would complain of excessive individualism, many had to assert their own individuality to
leave the homeland. Beginning with the earliest English settlers, most immigrants to the United States were, compared
to those left behind, risktakers. Although some were driven
to escape debtors' prisons in Britain, or hunger in Ireland, or
the inferno of Hitler's Germany, the vast majority of immigrants—even those from southern Italy or the Philippines

who never planned to remain—were willing to risk incredibly hard journeys to reach the strange new land called America. They were dissatisfied and courageous enough to uproot themselves from the soil which had nourished generations before them. They were willing to forgo the smells, sights, and sounds of their childhood. They were able to break with aunts, uncles, and cousins, and sometimes with brothers and sisters or parents to move to the New World. It is hard for Americans—whose small conjugal families are now so mobile and dispersive—to imagine the psychological risk-taking for men and women who ripped themselves away from the cohesive, extended families of eastern and southern Europe and Asia to journey to a faraway land whose language, religion, and customs would be strange. Once in America, from the Pilgrims of Massachusetts to the Mexicans of Texas, they tended to settle in small enclaves to perpetuate at least some aspects of the cultures of their homelands. But the decision to come often signified a declaration of independence from at least a portion of their own inheritance.

America was called the New World not only because of its relatively recent discovery, but because the men and women who went there usually were determined to lead new lives. Either they ambitiously sought economic opportunity which had been closed to them at home; or they wanted to practice a religion which had been persecuted; or they were running away from some trauma; or they were adventurers reaching for moonbeams; or they were political revolutionaries escaping oppression; or they were on the margin of starvation, hoping only to keep body and soul together. Whatever the reason, those who came *dared* to come. No matter how much they looked like the flotsam and jetsam of the Ukraine, Sicily, Shanghai, or London, the vast majority had that extra measure of salt in the blood which leads a man to turn his back on the known and face the unknown. Millions more than those who came thought about coming. Millions more wanted a better economic life, freedom for their religious beliefs and practices, and political liberty. Tens of thousands of young men and women thought, Should I become an indentured servant or not? Many thousands more wondered, Dare I leave the village? Some came; others did not. The difference was the *x* factor, that quality of psychological independence which many immigrants, particularly those from Jewish, Catholic, or Buddhist backgrounds, would resist in their own children.

In 1777, Michel Guillaume Jean de Crèvecoeur, an American immigrant farmer from France, wrote under the pseudonym of J. Hector St. John: "Every industrious European who transports himself here, may be compared to a sprout growing at the foot of a great tree; it enjoys and draws but a little portion of sap; wrench it from the parent roots, transplant it, and it will become a tree bearing fruit also." De Crèvecoeur overstated the process of acculturation for the first generation, particularly for later immigrants from southern and eastern Europe and Asia. Most immigrants drew heavily on the culture of their homelands, and tried to re-create as much of it as was compatible with the freedom and mobility of American life. But the immigrant saga did not stop with the first generation. It was the fruit born of the tree—the children for whose sake so many immigrants had uprooted themselves—who usually rushed headlong to embrace the cult of individualism taught by American schools, newspapers, books, magazines, and their peers. Immigrants usually wanted their children to achieve like good Americans, but they also wanted them to remain dependent on the family like good Germans, Italians, Chinese, and Jews. When the children forgot their obligations to the family and failed to respond to parental authority, there was much tongue-clucking and head-wagging. The children were behaving like crazy Americans. They had caught the fever of individualism. Anxious to be fully accepted in the Anglo-Saxon Protestant America of individualistic men and women, they often declared their independence sharply.

THE NEW ZION

Since the late eighteenth century, large numbers of Americans have not only believed in independence for themselves but they have promoted the ideal of liberty for others with messianic zeal. The powerful American sense of mission is the result of many forces, including the Protestant stress on personal salvation through renewal by the grace of God; the emphasis in pietistic, evangelical Protestantism on the promise of millennium through the second coming of Christ; the first rejection of Europe by Americans in revolution against England; and continued rejection of the ideologies of Europe by later immigrants. The earliest Puritans thought that New England was intended by God to be a new Zion for the promotion of spiritual freedom under his will, but by the time of the Revolution most Americans believed that the United States was intended by God to be a new Jerusalem in order to promote liberty in human (not just spiritual) affairs. John Adams wrote many years before the battle of Lexington that he considered the settlement of the American colonies "as the opening of a grand scene and design in Providence for the illumination of the ignorant and the emancipation of the slavish part of mankind all over the earth."

Many Americans had a growing sense of individual utopianism based on the power of independent choice by the advent of the war for independence. The Revolution was justified by Jefferson in the Declaration of Independence, not by asserting American nationality, but by emphasizing the inviolability of individual independence when he wrote in the first draft of the Declaration that it was "sacred and undeniable . . . that all men are created equal and independent." After the Revolution, tens of thousands of Americans were convinced that the mission of America was the celebration of individual freedom through the success of the American nation. "Our experiment," wrote Jefferson in 1787, "will be that men may be trusted to govern themselves without a master."

Henceforth, the mission of the United States was to spread the gospel of personal liberty. Turning their backs on what they saw as the corruption, orthodoxies, and hierarchies of Europe, many, including Washington in his Farewell Address, believed America could fulfill its mission of spreading liberty by perfecting it at home and avoiding entangling commitments with other governments. Sympathy and moral support were given to the nineteenth-century revolutions in Latin America and Europe, but neutrality and isolation was the prevailing policy of government. Missionary activity, concentrated on the peoples of Asia and the Pacific islands, was left mainly to sectarian Protestant denominations which were interested primarily in the liberation of the soul rather than political freedom. But the statesmen and poets of America seemed never to tire of recalling the promise of the Revolution. Lincoln called it "the germ which has vegetated, and still is to grow and expand into the universal liberty of mankind." Emerson wrote, "The office of America is to liberate."

The zeal of Americans for human regeneration in the nineteenth century found many expressions within North America, including crusades against Indians; Protestant revivalism; manifest destiny in the war against Mexico; anti-Catholicism; woman suffrage; the temperance movement; the founding of utopian communities; and the campaign to abolish slavery. Toward the end of the nineteenth century many Americans wrote and spoke of carrying their mission overseas. Under the influence of the evolutionary theories of Charles Darwin, some believed it was the right and duty of Anglo-Saxons (including North Europeans) to colonize the world. Professor John W. Burgess, a leading political scientist at Columbia University, wrote: "Since by far the larger part of the surface of the globe is inhabited by populations which have not succeeded in establishing civilized states, and since there is no human right to the status of barbarism, the Teutonic nations [sic] are called to carry the political civilization of the modern world into those parts of the world inhabited by un-political and barbaric races." Others believed that only English-speaking peoples were fit to lead. John Fiske, a leading historian, wrote in *Harper's* magazine in 1885 that "the work begun when the English race first colonized America is destined to go on until every land on the earth's surface that is not already the seat of an old civilization shall become English in its language, in its religion, in its political habits and tradition." Most Americans thought the job of spreading freedom was one for which Americans were best suited. Congregational minister Josiah Strong sounded a clarion call for Americans to Christianize the world. In his book *Our Country: Its Possible Future and Its Present Crisis,* written in 1885, Strong saw "the Anglo-Saxon, divinely commissioned to be his brother's keeper." Whereas forty years before, another Congregational minister, Horace Bushnell, had seen the charge of America "to present mankind a spectacle of . . . a religious nation, blooming in all the Christian virtues; the protector of the poor; the scourge of oppression; the dispenser of light; and the symbol to mankind of the ennobling genial power of righteous laws and a simple Christian faith," Strong believed it necessary to export the American mission "down upon Central America and South America, out upon the islands of the sea, over upon Africa and beyond." Senator Orville Platt, feeling the weight of America's obligation to perfect mankind, believed that the "same force that had once guided Pilgrim sails to Plymouth Rock had impelled American ships at Manila and Santiago." It fell to the United States, maintained Platt, to discharge "the duty of extending Christian civilization, crushing despotism, and making the rights of man prevail. . . . Providence has put it upon us and we propose to execute it."

EXPORTING AMERICANISM

Within a few years the call to extend America's mission through colonialism was put to a practical test. The United States defeated Spain in a war which had begun ostensibly over the issue of Spanish oppression in Cuba. Halfway around the world in Manila Bay, Commodore George Dewey's ships sank an obsolete Spanish squadron on the morning of May 1, 1898. Although Filipino insurgents had already captured most of the islands' major strategic centers from the Spanish, who had governed the Philippine Islands for nearly four hundred years, President William McKinley, who had asked for war against Spain "in the name of humanity, in the name of civilization," decided that the United States had an obligation to acquire the Philippines by force. He told a Methodist delegation at the White House that when he was uncertain as to what his course of action in the Philippines should be, he prayed for guidance. One night the revelation came. "There was nothing left for us to do but take them all," he said, "and to educate the Filipinos, and uplift and civilize and Christianize them [presumably he meant Protestantize, since the Philippines was already overwhelmingly Catholic], and by God's grace do the very best we could by them as our fellow men for whom Christ also died."

The burden assumed by McKinley for Americans was quickly taken up by thousands of public school teachers and Protestant missionaries. A call went out to the nation's teachers to volunteer for service in the newly created public school system of the Philippines. Two troopships arrived in 1901 with 1,400 American teachers, many of whom were just past twenty, imbued with the desire, as they said, to teach "self-reliance," "the dignity of labor," and "democracy." Of the 540 who arrived on the U.S. Army transport *Thomas,* and were later called "Thomasites," twenty-seven died of tropical diseases or met violent death at the hands of bandits during the first twenty months. Others who were disillusioned and discouraged by the problems of teaching in a strange culture left for home. But the vast majority of missionary-teachers remained for at least two years, and by 1902 there were 1,074 of them, constituting more than one third of the entire primary school teaching staff in the islands.

The Thomasites were products of the messianic spirit of the age. In 1886, one year after the publication of Josiah Strong's *Our Country,* a student conference was held at Northfield, Massachusetts, the base of operations of the influential evangelist Dwight L. Moody. Over one hundred students volunteered for foreign mission service, following the slogan "The evangelization of the world in this generation." The Student Volunteer Movement, which for the next three decades was to send additional thousands of college men and women to the far corners of the earth, was born. Following a Student Volunteer convention at Nashville, Tennessee, in 1906, a Presbyterian layman launched the Laymen's Missionary Movement to support the overseas work of the volunteers with dollars and cents. The enthusiasm of Americans to export plumbing, literacy, health, democracy, and Protestantism through the Student Volunteer Movement to the peoples of Asia lasted until the outbreak of World War I.

Although Americans were anxious to export liberty and education to the Philippines, they apparently were interested primarily in obtaining concessions and controlling markets in Latin America. The main responsibility of American statesmen in Latin America became the keeping of order. But keeping order was rarely justified in terms of protecting American property, at least not in major public speeches. To Theodore Roosevelt, Woodrow Wilson, Warren Harding, and Calvin Coolidge, order in Latin America was somehow equated with civilization and decency. Roosevelt warned that "a general loosening of the ties of civilized society . . . requires intervention by some civilized action, and in the western hemisphere . . . may force the United States, however reluctantly, in flagrant cases of such wrongdoing or impotence, to the exercise of an international police power." To an official British visitor, Woodrow Wilson once asserted, "I am going to teach the South American republics to elect good men." Franklin Roosevelt, later to author the United States good-neighbor policy toward Latin America, commenting in 1920 on his responsibilities as Assistant Secretary of the Navy under Wilson, remarked: "You know I have had something to do with the running of a couple of little republics. The facts are that I wrote Haiti's constitution myself, and if I do say it, I think it a pretty good constitution."

World War I provided Americans with an extraordinary opportunity for exercising moral fervor in international relations. Since the Revolution, Americans have defended their participation in wars in terms of messianic ideals rather than national, sectional, or economic interests. Thus, the invasion of Canada in 1812, instigated by the farmers of the Middle West, was undertaken to protect "freedom of the seas"; the attempt to expand slave territory through the conquest of Mexico was explained as "manifest destiny"; the Spanish-American War, fought in part to protect American investments, was justified by the widespread messianic desire to relieve the Cubans from Spanish despotism; and World War I, which involved the United States because of its strong interest in protecting the balance of power in Europe was fought "to make the world safe for democracy." In every case there was a substantial measure of truth to the rationalizations for participation in war. The missionary impulse, however misguided, was genuine in World War I no less than in the Revolution itself and in Woodrow Wilson, a stern Presbyterian moralist, as much as in Thomas Jefferson, a denominationally unaffiliated Deist.

At first Wilson saw no moral issue in the European war between Germany and the Allies. After American intervention, the conflict became the war "to make the world safe for democracy." As the President announced on the morning of the armistice: "Everything for which America fought has been accomplished. It will now be our fortunate duty to assist by example, by sober, friendly counsel, and by material aid in the establishment of just democracy throughout the world." Eight months later, when presenting the peace treaty and the League of Nations to the United States Senate, he maintained that the United States entered the war on a different basis from the European countries. "We entered it, not because our material interests were directly threatened or because any special treaty obligation to which we were party had been violated but only because we saw the supremacy and even the validity of right everywhere put in jeopardy and free government likely to be everywhere imperiled," the President explained. The high idealism and moral purpose of Wilson was not sustained by the American people or Congress, whose sense of mission in the 1920's lapsed considerably from its prewar height as a growing fun-morality competed increasingly with the sterner demands of Christian conscience.

MISSION AT HOME

Even those Americans who maintained a high sense of missionary devotion preferred the germ theory of Lincoln (liberty is contagious) to the view that the export of democracy through alliances and treaties was the business of the United States government. The disillusionment following World War I led to a revival of isolationism and concentration on domestic utopian schemes such as prohibition. America refused to enter the League of Nations and rejected the "corruptions" of Europe once again. Fundamentalist politicians, such as William Jennings Bryan, had always believed that America should perfect its mission at home rather than adventure abroad. Scandals over armaments profits proved to domestic reformers that a policy of isolation which kept America pure from the contamination of Europe was the best way to fulfill America's mission after all.

Bryan had made the western farmers' campaign for cheap

currency a moral issue by pleading to the leaders of his own party that they not crucify mankind on a cross of gold. Theodore Roosevelt, Woodrow Wilson, and Franklin Roosevelt clothed their programs of social reform in millennial slogans: "The Square Deal"; "The New Freedom"; and "The New Deal." Later John F. Kennedy and Lyndon B. Johnson, with no less sincerity, would employ the catchwords "The New Frontier" and "The Great Society."

Underlying these phrases is a persistent and confident belief in the ability of America to perfect its own society. At the worst period of the depression in 1931, with tens of millions of Americans suffering poverty, and when the prospects for recovery were grim, a committee of the American Historical Association concluded:

> The people of this country are engaged in no mere political experiment, as often imagined, but are attempting to build a civilization in a new natural setting, along original lines, with science and machinery as their great instrumentalities of work . . . underlying all these national ideas is a belief that . . . all legislation, all community action, all individual effort are founded on the assumption that evils can be corrected, problems solved . . . essentially by this fate is American civilization justified.

The obligation of national mission has engaged Americans in a continuing and almost neurotic quest for a sense of national purpose. It is one thing to assume the salvific powers of new Zion; it is quite another to have a plan for salvation. In any decade there are several books published which propose a plan for national salvation. At the medium-sized library at Brandeis University, I made a list of book titles issued from 1909 to 1938 aimed at giving content to America's self-appointed messianic role. Beginning with Herbert Croly's *The Promise of American Life,* they include *The New Democracy: America and the New Epoch; America and the New Era; America Faces the Future; New Frontiers;*

America Must Choose: America Must Act; American Purpose; and *America Now.* In 1944, Eric A. Johnston topped all titles with *America Unlimited.*

In 1942, with the advent of World War I, historian Charles A. Beard, with the help of his wife Mary, attempted to summarize the content of American mission in his book *The American Spirit.* Beard, who had lent his energetic mind and pen to populist and progressive crusades and to attacks on European decadence in defense of American isolationism, saw America as the hope of mankind. American civilization, he wrote, "embraces a conception of history as a struggle of human beings in the world for individual and social perfection—for the good, the true, the beautiful—against ignorance, disease, the harshness of physical nature, the forces of barbarism in individuals and in society . . . life ever engaged in a struggle for a decent and wholesome existence against the forces of barbarism and pessimism wrestling for possession of the human spirit."

WORLD WAR II

A world war once again focused America's sense of national mission. Franklin D. Roosevelt rallied Americans in a global struggle against despotic and tyrannical regimes. He made the war a crusade for the four freedoms: freedom from want, freedom from fear, freedom of religion, and freedom of speech. The four freedoms were Woodrow Wilson's "New Freedom" writ large and the Atlantic Charter and the United Nations repeated Wilson's vision of self-determination for nations in cooperative concert to prevent the scourge of war for all time. This time, the United States accepted its responsibility in a new League of Nations; but disillusionment in the aftermath of war was no less than it had been following World War I. Liberty did not spread although hundreds of thousands of Americans had been killed or wounded and billions of dollars had been spent in its behalf. America's mission focused effectively on the reconstruction of the defeated nations of Germany and Japan. Ancient traditions were uprooted; social structures were smashed; and social democracy and free enterprise were encouraged by legions of teachers, engineers, and civil servants. But Russian-style communism advanced to Berlin, and in China, long romanticized by Americans as a nation of smiling, friendly peasants amenable to Christianization and democracy, Communists also gained control.

The Communists also had a messianic vision for export which they militantly pressed wherever conditions permitted. The American Revolution had advanced the ideal of political and religious liberty through equality of opportunity; the twentieth-century Communist Revolution promoted the ideal of equality of condition over strict political controls (equality of opportunity, they said, was impossible under capitalism in Europe and America and feudalism in the underdeveloped countries). Both concepts were Western in their origin, and much of the world was indifferent to the ideological struggle which took form in the cold war. But the "loss of China," as Americans put it, was a terrible blow to the American psyche. It was followed by the frustrating, stalemated war in Korea and the capture of North Vietnam by Communists.

THE COLLAPSE OF PURPOSE

Everywhere American power and popularity seemed to be on the decline. Accounts of anti-American demonstrations and riots in Latin America, Africa, Korea, and Japan seared the cables of the international news services. The American Zion, far from being fulfilled despite the agony of two world wars, was on the defensive. The nation suffered what appears in retrospect to have been a nervous breakdown leading to the madness of McCarthyism. The Wisconsin senator promised to uproot the satanic, conspiratorial forces that had betrayed the mission of America, and millions of citizens were prepared to follow his lead. McCarthy was buried by his own intemperance and the courage of a handful of men who had retained their sanity, but the United States in the 1950's was still dismayed and bewildered by reports of declining American prestige among the peoples of Asia, Latin America, and Africa. The moral thunderbolts issued by Eisenhower's Secretary of State, John Foster Dulles, promising "liberation" to the peoples under communism, "the unleashing of Chiang Kai-shek," and "massive retaliation," reached new heights of messianic rhetoric in foreign relations but were unmatched by action of major consequence in Asia or Europe.

At home, great power apparently did not lead to self-respect either. A profusion of popular and sociological literature decrying the decline of the Protestant ethic of initiative and hard work were read and discussed with self-flagellating curiosity in the homes and college classrooms of the land. Americans were a "lonely crowd" of flabby, "other-directed," "status seekers" manipulated by "hidden persuaders," "taste makers," and "waste makers." It was clear that the vast wilderness of commodities which was America did not satisfy the spiritual or emotional hunger of millions.

THE UGLY AMERICAN

The vaunted American sense of purpose seemed to be floundering when there appeared on the scene a book, *The Ugly American,* by William J. Lederer and Eugene Burdick, which, as advertised in the paperback edition, purported to unmask "the blundering hypocrisy of some of our top-level diplomats," and to expose "the opportunism, incompetence and cynical deceit that have become embedded in the fabric of our public relations, not only in Asia but all over the world." The cause of declining American prestige and growing Communist power, according to Lederer and Burdick, was not, as McCarthy had maintained, the purposeful betrayal of American principles by devious and highly skilled Communist conspirators but materialistic, blunderbuss diplomats who had completely lost all sense of America's revolutionary mission to liberate mankind from the shackles of despotism and poverty. Too many American representatives in foreign lands were fools who had gone soft.

Several such fools lurched through the pages of *The Ugly American* from their air-conditioned offices to government limousines to PX's and commissaries to cocktail parties, without ever learning the local languages, meeting workers or peasants, or thinking through the problems of development. There was Ambassador Louis Sears, envoy to the fictional Asian country of Sarkhan, who was vain, pompous, and stupid. His insensitivity was matched by the Chief of Information for the ICA (now AID) in fictional Setkya, who drove his big red convertible over the sidewalks and who staggered through whopping parties "where he brags that every chunk of food and every drop of liquor, is from the good ole U.S.A. to Buddhists and Moslems who drink only fruit juice, water or milk." There was George Swift, Deputy Chief of Mission in Sarkhan, whose ignorance of local values and tradition and preoccupation with pleasing visitors from Washington caused a major setback to American-Sarkhanese relations.

Against these insensitive fools, the authors matched the Honorable Gilbert MacWhite, Sears's successor as Ambassador to Sarkhan (Sears had been unhappy in that hot, dusty country living among all those natives and was rewarded with a much-desired federal judgeship), and several amateur do-gooders who brought the spirit and competence of the American frontier to the villages of Asia. MacWhite was an intelligent Foreign Service officer whose "tongue never thickened" and "mind seldom dulled"; and his body was hard and muscular, because when he was in the States or England he played squash at least three times a week. But MacWhite, for all his knowledge of Marxist theory and practice, his ability to learn the Sarkhanese language in fifteen weeks, and his swift mastery of the strategic and tactical problems facing the United States in Southeast Asia, was not the major hero of the book. That honor fell to the amateurs, particularly to "the ugly American," Homer Atkins. Although he was worth three million dollars, "every dime of which he had earned by his own efforts," his fingernails were black with grease and his fingers bore tiny nicks and scars of a lifetime of practical engineering. He spoke with disdain of American technicians and diplomats: "Well, tell'm to get off their asses and out into the boondocks."

MacWhite put Atkins and his wife to work out in the boondocks, where they lived in a house with "pressed earth floors, one spigot of cold water, a charcoal fire, two very comfortable hammocks, a hoard of small, harmless insects, and a small, dark-eyed Sarkhanese boy about nine years old who apparently came with the house." Emma Atkins learned the language of the marketplace, loved her neighbors, and eventually invented a new broom handle to replace the reed with a short stem about two feet long that had been used for centuries and had bent the backs of the women of the village of Chang'dong. Homer joined forces with an improbable Sarkhanese young man named Jeepo, to create a makeshift pump out of native materials and to build a small but thriving industrial complex in Chang'dong.

Atkins was the prototype American hero—simple, direct, gregarious, self-reliant, a jack-of-all-trades, and a doer. There were other successful amateurs: John Colvin, who believed that if the people of Sarkhan could be taught to use milk and its by-products, their cattle would prosper on land that was otherwise useless and who was in Sarkhan completely on his own; Father John X. Finian, who survived terrible attacks of dysentery, learned the Sarkhanese language, and helped the Sarkhanese to organize effective counterinsurgency forces; Edwin B. Hillandale, the "rag-time kid," a slender U.S. Air Force colonel with red hair, who rode a motorcycle and charmed the Filipinos with his harmonica, the Sarkhanese with his knowledge of palmistry, and both with the enormous gusto with which he devoured their food; and Tom Knox, who drove his jeep into the countryside of Cambodia where, as a chicken farmer from Iowa, he won a reputation for working magic with chickens and sharply increasing the production of eggs. (He "picked up a few tricks that ah'm goin' to pass along to you.")

Except for Finian, the heroes of *The Ugly American* were not preoccupied with ideology. Knox came to Cambodia, he said, because "I just like people and chickens, and besides I wanted to get away from the farm for a year or so." Hillandale was never happier than when sitting in a Filipino restaurant, alternately playing his harmonica and washing down huge quantities of *adobo* and *pancit* and rice with cheap Filipino rum. They were not theoretically inclined, but were interested in practical matters: cow's milk, canned vegetables, pumps, broom handles, and chicken eggs. They were adaptable, learned new languages, ate new foods, and braved physical hardships. They loved to work, but they believed their mission in life was to free others from arduous oppression, including the heavy burden of backbreaking labor. They preached the dignity of work and the independence of man, and had no doubts that these values would be adopted by the villagers of Asia if presented honestly and with respect for local dances, ceremonies, food, and language (not seen as related to authoritarianism or poverty).

The authors presented their frontier-type Americans as the answer to declining United States prestige in Southeast Asia and the answer to economic development in Asia. Whenever Asians spoke from the heart in *The Ugly American*, they praised Homer Atkins and deplored Lou Sears. They asked, as did one man described as the best-known journalist in Burma, for Americans as they are in the United States, "wonderfully friendly, unassuming, and interested in the world." They complained about pretentious living overseas in golden ghettos and praised (as did the fictional journalist) a Burmese-speaking couple, who showed the natives how to can fruit and vegetables and distributed high-quality seeds to help organize a community canning cooperative. "I believe firmly that the Americans could drive the Communists out of Asia in a few years if you really tried and were willing to live out here on our level," said the journalist. When asked what he would do to help bolster American prestige and power in Asia, he replied: "I would send more people like the Martins to Burma. That's all you need. You could forget about the hordes of executives, PX's, commissaries, and service forces which are now needed to support the Americans abroad. And then, of course, you could save many of the millions of dollars Americans seem to think essential to any aid program." The Burmese concluded his advice to Ambassador MacWhite: "But most important— act like Americans. We love Americans—the kind we meet in America."

Evidently there were many Americans who appreciated the message. The Ugly American, first issued in July, 1958, was a Book-of-the-Month Club selection in October and by November had gone through twenty printings. Five years after its first appearance, it had been given thirteen large printings in its paperback edition and had been made into a popular motion picture. The Ugly American was a call for a restatement and purification of mission which spoke to the anxieties of many Americans. The authors concluded their book: "We have so lost sight of our own past that we are trying to sell guns and money alone, instead of remembering that it was the quest for the dignity of freedom that was responsible for our own way of life."

THE BIRTH OF THE PEACE CORPS

The publication of The Ugly American stimulated discussion among college professors, ministers, and congressmen about the creation of a corps of young men and women volunteers who would carry the germ of liberty with them to the villages of underdeveloped countries and help to teach the skills required for economic development. The idea was discussed in the campaign headquarters of both presidential candidates in 1960, and on November 2, 1960, the Democratic candidate, John F. Kennedy, promised to begin a volunteer Peace Corps of "the best Americans we can get to speak for our country abroad." A minority was skeptical, especially those who wished they had proposed the idea first, but most Americans warmly accepted the proposal. Here was a way the United States could explain itself to the world and help others at the same time.

The Peace Corps, as conceived by President Kennedy, would proclaim to the world that Americans had lost neither their idealism nor their vigor. It would correct the image held by countless numbers of Africans, Asians, and Latins of Americans as materialistic, effete, and insensitive. It might even stimulate other overseas agencies—AID, USIS, and embassy personnel—to learn languages, study cultures, and live less ostentatiously.

R. Sargent Shriver, the Peace Corps's first director, lobbied for the plan in Congress with unembarrassed zeal and unusual success. In the first debate on the Peace Corps bill in August and September, 1961, dozens of congressmen proclaimed the Peace Corps as a historic fulfillment of American mission. "What could be more magnificent than sending well-prepared and useful Americans to other lands to help teach and train people there for a better life?" queried Senator Frank Moss of Utah. "The missionary," he said, "is dedicated to the spreading of the philosophy of religion while the Peace Corps man must be dedicated, among other things, to spreading a philosophy of government . . . acquainting the people of other countries, and particularly of the underdeveloped countries, in which freedom is new and raw, of the basic concepts of America through contact with our most effective apostles, our American youth." Moss urged that "we must make them understand that the fruits of self-government are far superior to those of an authoritarian state, and we must make them realize that, in choosing the direction they will take, it will be wisest and most rewarding to walk in the ways of freedom." He concluded, "All of this we can do while we teach health, agriculture, and the three R's."

Senator Hubert Humphrey of Minnesota spoke of the Peace Corps as exemplifying "the real spirit of our country. It would prove to Khrushchev and the world that America is not going soft." Senator Ralph Yarborough of Texas told Peace Corps trainees in his state that they were a "chosen few" who represented "American idealism at a new peak." They were, he said, missionaries who carried "the true spirit of America in your hearts." Senator Stephen Young of Ohio saw the volunteers as men and women of goodwill who "must have the zeal of hardy missionaries . . . by example, they must win friends for America and our way of life." Senator Stuart Symington of Missouri looked at the Peace Corps bill and concluded that "there is nothing better than to have young Americans spread the doctrine of free enterprise, and carry abroad word of what our country stands for."

Senator Estes Kefauver of Tennessee viewed the Peace Corps as "something which accords with our national character . . . helping people on a person-to-person basis with whatever help is needed." If the world gets a misleading picture of America, said Kefauver, it is because the people who represent us abroad are not usually the "plain people" of whom Lincoln spoke. "We need more plain people to carry our story to plain people elsewhere in the world—people who can farm and can teach others to farm; carpenters who can build and who can help others learn the art; and teachers and nurses and managers of small industries who can likewise encourage others in distant lands to make a better life for themselves and their neighbors." His colleague Senator Gale McGee from Wyoming also bemoaned the false image which others had of America. They have failed to see that "we have been a nation of men with ideas, . . . dedicated to the fundamental principle that all men are free . . . among the new nations which aspire to the twin goals of independence and individual freedom we have found, in our contacts around the world, that the youth of America serve perpetually as the finest ambassadors of American ideas." Senator Frank Church of Idaho agreed: "When we send young Americans who believe strongly in free institutions, who are trained to do useful and constructive work in the newly emerging countries . . . we will be sending young ambassadors of our own way of life," he said.

The debate in the House of Representatives struck similar themes to those recorded in the Senate: "a renewal of the spirit that made our country great, a renewal of the spirit of the pioneers"; "a means of answering the Communist charge that America is soft to the people around the world"; "convey to these people the value of a free society"; "the opportunity to help in explaining the ideas and ideals which have made us what we are today"; "appeals to both the idealistic and pragmatic qualities of the indomitable American spirit." The Peace Corps was praised mainly by Democrats and liberals, but also by Republicans and conservatives. It was seen by many, even at the outset, as an exemplary expression of American values and character.

THE MANY MEANINGS OF THE PEACE CORPS

For the next several years, the Peace Corps was to provide psychic income for millions of Americans. As the reports came in on volunteers who lived self-sufficiently in the boondocks, and who invented ingenious devices and techniques for improving the agriculture or health of their hosts while adapting to local conditions, Americans became increasingly proud of the Peace Corps and increasingly anxious to see only the fulfillment of their hopes in it. By the second year of its operation, conservative Republican congressmen were praising the Peace Corps for, as Representative Edwin Durno of Oregon put it, "exporting Americanism." I recall a conversation at an embassy party in Manila in 1962, not more than a year after the first Peace Corps volunteers had arrived in the field (a year of many mistakes, difficulties, and even tragedy), where I met a well-known and extremely conservative political leader from the east coast who thrust a hand at me for a hearty shake, exclaiming: "You're the Peace Corps man. Isn't that wonderful!" When I explained that there were a few problems in our organization just like everywhere else, the rejoinder came: "You can't kid me. The Peace Corps is simply marvelous."

The Peace Corps was marvelous, but for reasons which the embassy visitor never dreamed. The volunteers were fulfilling the objectives of congressional leaders who steered the Peace Corps Act through Congress. They were "willing to serve, under conditions of hardship if necessary," to help other countries meet their needs for trained manpower, to promote better understanding of the American people, and to encourage a more thorough understanding of other people by Americans. A research study[1] made in the Philippines three years later by social scientists under contract to the Peace Corps would show that the volunteers in the earliest groups, despite their misgivings, provided effective help in teaching English and science and promoted a favorable image of America. There could be no question that they were gaining a more thorough understanding of Filipinos and their culture than any previous group of Americans had done.

Beyond these three objectives, the volunteers were learning something which had never been discussed in Congress. They were learning about themselves as individuals and Americans. They were learning how much of what they had taken as universally good, true, and beautiful were the values of a peculiar culture and people shaped by historical circumstances which had been extremely different from those experienced by others in the world, and especially different from the peoples of Asia. They learned this not as anthropologists, observing and taking notes with clinical detachment, but as young men and women striving for a surer sense of themselves while attempting to live out the ideals of Ameri-

[1] *Referred to in Chapter 5.*

can culture in relationship with people who, at the deeper levels of emotional life, did not share those ideals. Peace Corps volunteers were not just studying another culture; they were forced to come to terms with it in daily contact with children, teachers, neighbors, and in the marketplace. They learned in the process—not just new skills or even the languages and customs of other people—that as Americans they were a peculiar people. Deep in their feelings, even though they could rarely articulate them, many began to understand the strong drives for independence, achievement, and mission which brought them to the barrios.

Of all the things that can be said of the Peace Corps— its inestimable propaganda value, its worth in helping to promote economic development, and the formal skills and knowledge acquired by volunteers—none is more important than this: young men and women tested and stretched themselves in a complex, self-revealing, and often painful adventure in human relationships which led to an acute emotional awareness of their Americanness.

Tests administered to volunteers headed for the Philippines at their training site at Penn State University showed that they were not typical Americans. Three major motivations shaped their decision to join the Peace Corps, apart from private reasons: an altruistic desire to help others; a patriotic concern for America's welfare and prestige; and a desire to learn from new experience. The tests also revealed that volunteers tended not to care about pecuniary gain, and that they were not usually interested in business or scientific careers. To Filipino nationalists in Manila, who saw Americans as materialistic, selfish, and exploitative, the volunteers were peculiar Americans because they were interested in Filipino culture and history and willing to share physical hardship to help others. To Filipino teachers and farmers in the provinces, whose ideas of Americans come mainly from movies and stories about the behavior of soldiers who liberated the Philippines in World War II, the unusually conscientious, hard-working and serious Peace Corps volunteers also seemed peculiar because they were different from other Americans. But in a larger sense the volunteers were peculiar not because they were special Americans, but because they were quintessential Americans in exemplifying the dominant values of American culture: personal independence, achievement, and mission.

Eventually many of them saw themselves not so much as deviants within their own culture, but, from the Asian point of view, as representatives of a strange culture. Most Americans, they realized, at least most in the ever-widening middle classes, whether they were conservatives or liberals, idealists or cynics, Catholics, Jews, or Protestants, Negroes or white men, engineers or lathe operators, were planful, organized, hurried, restless consumers of time who were driven incessantly to accomplish task upon task.

ON THEIR OWN

Whatever personal reasons they had for volunteering—a chance to get away from overly domineering or protective parents, a chance at personal romance and marriage, time to gain greater understanding of oneself, postponement of career choice, a reaction against lectures and books, and a desire to see the world—the single strongest unifying motivation of volunteers appears to have been the desire to improve the world *as individuals on their own*. In this they were no different from Tom Knox, John Colvin, or Homer Atkins in *The Ugly American*. Nor did they differ in their convictions as to how the world could be improved. Better health, more food, more democracy, and education. These were the prerequisites for the ultimate good of personal freedom, the supreme value of American culture, which volunteers, along with the vast majority of their fellow Americans, believed to be America's unique contribution to the world. "To every man, regardless of his birth, a shining golden opportunity, to every man the right to live, to work, to be himself, and to become whatever thing his manhood and his vision can combine to make—this, seeker, is the promise of America," wrote Thomas Wolfe. The heroes of *The Ugly American* and most Peace Corps volunteers would have agreed.

Despite the widespread acceptance of labor unions, social security, and other aspects of the welfare state, most Americans still valued independence in the middle of the twentieth century. In fact, the advances made under the New Deal and subsequent welfare programs were justified in terms of expanding equality of opportunity to make it possible for independence to be realized by larger numbers of Americans. The concept of equality of opportunity has always been concomitant to the value of personal independence which, by making achievement the measure of individual worth, implies also that everyone should start life at roughly the same base line.

Notwithstanding the recent vast literature on conformity in American life, Americans in 1960 valued independence as much or more than their forefathers. Americans have always been acquiescent in the authority of the marketplace, as every astute observer since de Tocqueville has noted, precisely because they were raised to be independent of the authority of state, church, and family in making choices. The more free individuals are from those traditional guides, the more significant are cliques, clubs, associations, and mass media. Far from being incompatible with conformity in matters of fashion, morals, and opinion, the tendency toward independence in choice of friends, mates, and jobs creates a problem of adjustment and militates toward popular or fashionable as opposed to traditional conformity. In America, the price of independence from tradition in some matters has always been conformity to the marketplace in others. But the same pressures which made for independence in the eighteenth and nineteenth centuries have been intensified: valuing of individual choice (for women and children more than ever), advancing technology, and urbanization. The same culture heroes are worshiped: the independent pioneers (including spacemen), always on the move, performing feats of daring; the lonesome cowboys, unencumbered even by family ties; the athletes whose extraordinary feats can be measured in the latest recorded percentages; and the completely self-sufficient modern gunfighter from Humphrey Bogart to Secret Agent 007.

Individualism is still an American cult. Personal independence remains the dominant value of the culture, and the assertion of self its main requirement, as mothers preoccupied with separating squabbling siblings at dinnertime can testify. A study of the values of American college students in 1957 found that the great majority of students were "unabashedly self-centered," a conclusion which was supported by the results of a comparative study of American students and those from Canada, India, China, Japan, and Norway, which showed that "orientation to self" as opposed to "orientation to society" was strongest among Americans.

The earliest Peace Corps volunteers were often self-selected apostles of their own cultural values, although many had rejected elements of their culture for not living up to those values. Even more than most college students, they valued personal independence and achievement. Much more than most, they believed in America's historic mission to spread the value of freedom of choice. In this, the Peace Corps volunteers in the Philippines received considerable encouragement from me and my staff. While I always emphasized the importance of appreciation, respect, understanding, and even empathy for Filipinos and their own culture, I also repeatedly stressed, as in one speech in Manila, that "the Peace Corps in the Philippines believes in change for ourselves as well as those with whom we work and live, change in the direction of greater autonomy and self-motivation for the individual." I once told the volunteers and Filipinos that "to encourage the free, creative spirit of the children and neighbors with whom we come in contact is our greatest challenge."

More important than what members of the staff in the

Philippines had to say was the inspirational force of President Kennedy's words that "now as never before, hundreds of millions of men and women—who had formerly believed that stoic resignation in the face of hunger and disease and darkness was the best one could do—have come alive with a new sense that the means are at hand with which to make for themselves a better life." More than most Americans, the volunteers agreed with President Kennedy that it is "the American people who should be marching at the head of this worldwide revolution." In his inaugural address the President had pledged America's best efforts "to those people in the huts and villages of half the globe struggling to break the bonds of mass misery . . . to help them help themselves."

ASKING QUESTIONS

The heroes of *The Ugly American* anticipated President Kennedy's call and Peace Corps volunteers answered it. But there was a vast difference in what happened to the two groups of apostles. The men of *The Ugly American* never doubted the validity of their mission, their capacity to fulfill it (if not interfered with by heavy-footed foreign service officers), or the overwhelming desire of Asians to embrace it. The experience of Peace Corps volunteers was different. A girl from South Carolina wrote, "I sort of had the feeling that everyone wanted to be American and if given the chance, they would jump at it." Within six months, she knew better. Within two years, most volunteers questioned almost every important value they had learned from childhood, which means they questioned the bases for their own individual identities.

For some the questioning was deep; for others, relatively superficial. But they questioned and searched for answers and the nature of their mission changed in the process. It was not just the promotion of freedom through economic and political development, although it never stopped being that in part. The mission of the volunteers became more personal and less global. It was based not merely on awareness of the health and productivity gaps between the prosperous and the poor nations, but often on an acute understanding of the complexity and anguish of man's condition regardless of his background, wealth, color, or religion. The belief in individual freedom and of the special responsibility of the United States for spreading it did not die, but it became a part of larger, if somewhat vaguer, understanding of both the limitations and the requirements as well as the strengths and potentialities of freedom. In their growing ability to comprehend their peculiarities as Americans, Peace Corps volunteers were ahead not just of Americans but of the vast majority of the peoples of the world who only dimly perceive the relationship of their personal identity to culture.

II
The "non-job"

: The United States and the Philippines have had a special and close relationship for more than half a century. After American forces took Manila in 1900, and (from a Filipino point of view) betrayed the national revolution by conquering the Filipino rebels, the United States established a colonial regime which was probably more popular than any other in the world. Early American colonial administration, despite insensitivity and bumbling, was in many respects a model for its time. Good roads were built. The latest public health measures were widely introduced. A public school system based on the English language was established and schools were built in the remotest barrios.

THE AMERICAN IMAGE IN THE PHILIPPINES

From the beginning, Americans established a policy of early independence for the Philippines. Three Filipinos served on the first governing commission headed by Governor William Howard Taft, and a Filipino was named the first Chief Justice of the Supreme Court. Elective government was instituted in municipalities in 1902, and the franchise was steadily liberalized. After Woodrow Wilson became President in 1913, the policy of Filipinization was advanced speedily. In seven years the number of Americans in the insular government was reduced from 2,600 to 582. In 1907 the Filipino House of Representatives became elective; nine years later the Senate followed, and both houses were given substantial control over appropriations.

Filipinization did not necessarily mean more efficient government. Nor did it lead to a better life for the people of the villages who constituted more than 90 percent of the Filipino population. Nor were American motives in extending self-government based purely on abstract liberal ideology. American anticolonialism was reinforced by sugar, dairy, and other domestic pressure groups anxious to end Filipino competition. The result of such pressures was legislation passed by Congress in 1934 spelling out terms of independence for the Philippines, including the right of Filipinos to control their domestic affairs for ten years as a commonwealth under the United States before achieving complete sovereignty.

Successive waves of American colonial governors, administrators, teachers, and missionaries left an image of Americans as powerful, rich, friendly, and beneficent. That picture was re-created when General Douglas MacArthur returned to the island of Luzon in 1944 to liberate the Filipinos from Japanese control. Early Spanish rulers had been ruthless, but the Japanese military occupation matched the worst periods of the Spanish regime for brutality. The American occupation in the first decade of the century had been compared favorably by Filipinos to the Spanish rule which preceded it; now American infantrymen were welcomed for having driven out the hated Japanese. The liberating GIs, joined by thousands of Filipinos who fought with them, often without pay, in comradely, fraternal alliance, were usually noisy and insensitive, but they were full of fun, friendly, and generous with candy and cigarettes.

Independence came after the war with the formal inauguration of the Philippine Republic on July 4, 1946. The country had been devastated. The Japanese had destroyed government offices, schools, and churches in all the major islands. Transportation and telecommunication facilities were in disarray. In Manila, 80 percent of the city had been blasted, mostly by American shells and bombs. Commerce was stalled and staples were scarce. Disease, including the once destroyed malaria, was rampant, but drugs were in short supply. Filipinos looked to their powerful *compadre*, Uncle Sam, for help; and during the first five postwar years the United States spent more than 2 billion dollars to assist the Philippines, including approximately 520 million dollars for war damage payments, and 250 million dollars to civilian employees of the United States Army. In 1951 the United States Economic Cooperation Administration at the Philippines began operations, and during the next ten years approximately 1 billion dollars more came to the Philippines in the form of payments to veterans, grants, loans, wages to civilian personnel, and other forms of assistance. To Filipinos, the United States appeared as a gigantically powerful and rich sponsor and protector. In return, Filipinos gave many important concessions to the United States. Pursuant to a 1947 agreement, the United States kept important air, naval, and other military bases in the archipelago, including the 150,000-acre reservation at Clark Air Force Base, only a few hours' drive from Manila. The Philippine Trade Act of 1946 provided for a period of free or preferential exports to the United States and for Americans in the Philippines to enjoy the same rights and privileges as Filipinos in the exploitation of natural resources and the operation of public services.

During the 1950's many Filipinos expressed a dissatisfaction with the agreement on bases and trade. Grumbling over American privileges was widespread in intellectual circles and in certain newspapers. But the vast majority of Filipinos and most officials in both Filipino major political parties continued to believe that the United States and the Philippines should maintain their special relationship. Filipinos would give loyalty and favors to Americans; the United States would give economic and technical assistance and military protection in return.

THE RETURN OF THE THOMASITES

When the Peace Corps was organized in Washington, it was believed by many that the Philippines would be the best place to begin a large program. It was reasoned that there would be few government-to-government problems; Filipinos in the barrios, holding Americans in high esteem, would welcome volunteers with grand hospitality; and volunteers would have less trouble in a culture which had long been exposed to Western, and especially American, influences.

What would the volunteers do? Washington officials and Filipino educators argued for a Peace Corps program which would help upgrade English teaching and introduce new techniques for teaching the recently adopted science and mathematics curricula. The quality of English instruction had declined because of the interruption of education during the war, the elimination of the seventh grade in the elementary school, the shortening of class hours, the dearth of textbooks, overcrowded classes, and because native speakers of the English language no longer taught in the elementary schools as Americans had done in the days of the Thomasites.

English was the language of instruction in the Filipino

public schools from the third grade on, but in actual practice, a minority of Filipino teachers frequently reverted to the local dialect in the classroom, and nearly all teachers and children avoided English outside of class. A 1960 study by a group of Filipinos and American educators showed that the English comprehension and speaking ability of both sixth-graders and second-year high school students in the year 1947 were far below comparable groups tested in 1925. The need for better English instruction was more pressing than ever. The relatively small but growing group of new entrepreneurs, managers, and technicians had learned their skills through English, but their replacements would have to know English too, as would clerks, secretaries, and skilled and semiskilled laborers.

The upgrading of spoken and written English had been a policy of American and Filipino governments for a number of years. The AID (then ICA) Education Division had supported the training of Filipino English teachers at the University of California in Los Angeles and had helped to prepare materials and tools for language training at the University of the Philippines and the Philippine Normal College in Manila. Also, the Rockefeller Foundation supported the Philippine Center for Language Study, which sponsored Filipino teachers for training at U.C.L.A. in the teaching of English as a second language.

AID officials endorsed and helped work out the concept of Peace Corps volunteers as educational aides to serve as models of spoken English. Since there were many unemployed teachers in the Philippines, the volunteers were not permitted to come as full-fledged teachers. Because most of them would be liberal arts graduates, there was even some question as to whether they would qualify as teachers. The answer to the dilemma of providing teaching help in English, science, and mathematics without supplying teachers was the amorphous job concept of educational aide. Volunteers would assist teachers but would not have their own classes.

The government of the Philippines asked that volunteers be assigned to small rural barrios consisting of from a dozen to a few hundred families. Many volunteers lived in barrios of *poblaciones,* the seats of government for the municipalities, the Philippine equivalent of counties in the United States. Here they met more highly educated and affluent persons—lawyers, doctors, traveling salesmen, and government officials—than could be found ordinarily in rural barrios. But a majority of volunteers were located in poor rice-growing and fishing villages remote from larger cities, although they often were close to or in towns.

When I visited volunteers, I was impressed by the extraordinary topographical and ethnic diversity of the Philippines. Although the Philippines consists of 7,100 islands, approximately 466 of which are occupied, its land surface roughly equals the size of the New England states and New York combined, nearly two thirds of which is on the two largest islands of Luzon and Mindanao, at the northern and southern ends of the archipelago. There are nine other major islands, and volunteers were eventually assigned to them all and to more than a dozen others, including tiny islands in the Sulu Archipelago, only a short sail from Borneo. On Luzon, they worked (among other places) in the high, rugged mountains which reached nearly 10,000 feet in Mountain Province and in the shadow of Mount Mayon, one of the world's most perfect volcanic cones, near the old port city of Legaspi. On Mindanao, the frontier island of the south, where the largest contingent of volunteers was assigned, they lived around the rim of 2,200-foot-high Lake Lanao, a tropical Lake Geneva which fills the cone of a vast extinct volcano, in the fertile Cotabato plains, the beautiful Agusan River valley, and in the rolling grasslands of Bukidnon plateau.

They lived and worked among more than a dozen distinct linguistic groups. Approximately 88 percent of the population is composed of the eight largest of these groups—Tagalog, Iloco, Bikol, Pampangan, Pangasinan, Cebuano, Hiligaynon, and Waray-Waray—and most volunteers worked with one of these so-called "majority" or "typical" Filipino groups. But others lived with minorities, particularly the Muslims of Mindanao. There, they taught the children of the Tao Suug (or land Muslims of the Sulu Archipelago) and of the Samals (or sea Muslims whose sailing vintas moved in the rapid currents of the Sulu Sea). They lived with the Magindanos of the large province of Cotabato and the Maranaos around Lake Lanao. The fewer than one out of ten volunteers who lived with Muslims (less than 5 percent of the Philippine population) became familiar with white-turbaned sultans in colorful togas, religious courts, polygamy, and even slavery. But the majority of volunteers who worked in the lowland Christian regions of the Philippines probably never heard the Darangan or warrior ballads of the Maranaos or talked with the sea gypsies known as the Badjaos, who lived by fishing, searching for turtle eggs, and by trading with land people in the islands of the Sulu Sea.

Most volunteers lived in the less exotic but at least as complex culture of the lowland Philippines. It was based mainly on the iron civilization of Malayan migrants who came to the Philippines from two hundred to three hundred years before Christ and who introduced and advanced lowland agriculture, weaving, pottery making, and glass- and metalworking. The culture of the Malays was added to by Arab and Indian merchants who reached the Philippines about the beginning of the Christian era and who in some instances settled in the islands for almost a thousand years. Later the Chinese established colonies along the coast and in the cities. Following Ferdinand Magellan's discovery of the islands in 1521, Spanish colonizers, hoping to find wealth in gold and silver, established a powerful colonial administration throughout most lowland central areas during the sixteenth century. In Mindanao and Sulu, the leaders of Muslim Malayans, the sultans, whose people had been converted to Islam centuries before, successfully resisted the Spanish forces. Elsewhere most Filipinos accepted Catholicism intermingled with traditional beliefs in spirits and ghosts.

Whether in the lowlands, the mountains, or in Muslim areas, the barrios of the Philippines were usually poor. Students often came to school hungry and dressed in torn clothes, or they did not come at all because they lacked the money to buy a pencil or paper. Even in the more prosperous barrios of the Visayas (the central islands) or Luzon, electricity and toilet facilities were rare. Everywhere pigs roamed freely, defecating where they chose. Public health measures were virtually nonexistent or only halfheartedly undertaken. Respiratory infections were rampant, and open sores on the bodies of schoolchildren or stray dogs were common.

In the barrios, volunteers were conscious of the sounds of humanity—grunting, snoring, crying, laughing—everpresent humanity amidst chickens, pigs, and dogs living and dying in the rhythmic ebb and flow of barrio existence. A family with a half dozen to a dozen children was often crowded into two or three rooms. Babies were constantly being born; but young and old people were constantly dying.

BARRIO DAYS

Despite the geographic and linguistic variety of the Philippines, there was a sameness to the quiet rhythm of life and death in the barrios. To pick a typical day of any one volunteer would not be misleading for the majority of them. Awakened at 6 A.M. by the crowing of the cock, the ringing of church bells, the shouts of a passing peddler on the way to the market, Ralph (to give him a name), his housemate or his helper (most volunteers lived with another volunteer and a Filipino or Filipina who helped with the cooking and housework) breakfasted on a little rice, perhaps an egg, coffee, and some fruit which was often plentiful (especially

bananas, but also papayas, mangoes, and coconuts). Except
in a few cases where the household helper was an ingenious
cook or where the local markets drew from a nearby larger
población or major city, there was little variety at breakfast
or any other meal. Morning was the best time for marketing
since the few fresh fish, chickens, or eggs might be sold before the sun was very high. Ralph sauntered to the marketplace for what was usually a pleasant bartering session. At
first he was dismayed by the complexities of haggling. Used
to the fixed prices of the United States, he was not a skillful
bargainer, although he began to enjoy his progress at bartering as time went on. (One group of volunteers cornered the
chicken market for about a month by inadvertently paying
twice the going rate until they discovered the reason for the
mounting resentment of their barrio neighbors.)

Ralph left for school shortly after breakfast. On Tuesdays
and Thursdays he had a special assignment at a barrio
school six miles from his barrio and he usually took a bus
most of the distance. For most volunteers the trip to school
meant a short walk down a dusty or muddy road, depending
upon whether it was the rainy or dry season. On the way,
they saw squawking chickens and snorting pigs, young men
already drinking *tuba* (fermented coconut juice) near the
sari-sari store (small, general purpose), children with
laughing, glistening faces who jumped and twisted and
kicked cans or dogs, and the endlessly curious, smiling faces
of women in the windows of nipa (palm thatch) houses.

Once in school, Ralph exchanged amenities with the principal and teachers. His task for the morning was to take over
a science unit in the fourth grade and later to help the coteacher prepare her lesson plan in English pronunciation. By
midmorning he was feeling underused and slightly bored. At
merienda (snacktime) he ate cassava cake and rice cake,
drank coffee, and tried to answer the teacher's questions
about Hollywood, General MacArthur, divorce in America,
war-damage claims, and birth control. Sometimes, especially
in later months, the teachers would talk also about English,

science, and arithmetic, but today the questions were banal. Ralph asked questions too. He wanted to know whether the teachers really respected the principal. What was their opinion as to how he should handle the boys who drank too much *tuba* and sometimes threw rocks at his house; why was there only one rice crop each year; what was the word or phrase in the dialect for punctuality?

Merienda over, Ralph went back to a classroom to show maps of far-off places to third-graders and to try to convince some of them that there were other countries in the world besides the United States, the Philippines, and Japan. In a few weeks Ralph planned to work with the sixth-grade science teacher in building model scales of the solar system. Here in the barrio school, he worked with only three of the six teachers. His housemate, Bill, assisting every day in the larger central school of the *población,* worked with a dozen.

With school over, Ralph waited for the bus to take him home. A few volunteers, he knew, had to paddle a small boat—one navigated six miles of water every day—and that was more exciting than waiting for or riding buses. But most of those who traveled any distance relied on the extraordinarily colorful and ingenious Filipino buses and jeepnies (jeeps made over in inimitable Filipino fashion to serve as small taxi-buses). Buses played a major part in the lives of volunteers: waiting for buses, dodging buses, and squeezing into buses even when it seemed impossible for another person to find two inches of sitting or standing room. This Tuesday the bus twisted and raced down rut-filled roads like a roller coaster at forty or fifty miles an hour, careening past carabao-drawn carts, jangling through tiny barrios, and Ralph was jarred up and down by wooden seats as he and his companions swayed with each turn. Inside the bus, men, women, and babies waited good-naturedly for their turn to get off, while atop the roof lay a cargo of chickens, firewood, and baggage; and beneath the floorboards pigs sent up a chorus of complaints as they jostled among heavy sacks of rice and corn.

Home from the bus ride, Ralph stopped for a Coke (Bill preferred beer) at the *sari-sari* store and for a chat with a neighboring farmer. Such talks were quiet, leisurely, inconsequential, but often pleasurable. The day before, Ralph had rushed home to work on a water-sealed toilet for his own house. Today he promised to lend some books from his library to a child who lived nearby. Children often came to his house in the afternoon to read or play, and Ralph and Bill loved the inquisitive, shy, black-haired, brown-eyed youngsters. On the way home, Ralph stopped to watch a funeral procession headed toward the cemetery. His eye caught the procession in a series of pictures: a small box covered with bright-colored paper carried by a boy or man; next to him, another man with a shovel over his right shoulder; then an expressionless young woman shuffling slowly to the cemetery. A few men dug a hole, and the little box was slipped into it. Two candles were lighted and put in the ground above the box, and then, with a quick motion of the hands from the head, across the chest to the abdomen, the women shuffled back to the road, a baby clasped to her breast and another small child tugging behind.

Ralph had a sudden impulse to go fishing, but he was two hundred miles from the nearest fishing waters. He had heard that other volunteers in fishing towns went spearfishing in the late afternoon. Some even fished at night with the help of a petromax lantern. One of his best friends from training, Len, went coral fishing regularly with a net, and sometimes fished off the beach with a hook and line. When he visited Len during Christmas, they watched from a small boat while the local fishermen dynamited and poisoned fish.

Down the road Ralph could see children already milling around his house. It was a typical Peace Corps house of open-frame construction with a nipa roof. Some Peace Corps houses were made entirely of nipa or *kogon* (grass) for the roof and bamboo for the frame, but this one was more substantial. It was a rented house, like most Peace Corps houses in the Philippines, although sometimes it was necessary for the Peace Corps to build houses, as in Mindanao, where more than eighty were constructed. Few had running water, but this one, like most, had a pump in the kitchen from which Ralph and Bill were able to draw water from a nearby well. Most of the houses had no electricity, but Ralph and Bill were lucky because they had it for several hours almost every evening.

Inside the house, Ralph was impressed with how much of a home it had actually become. The boys had built shelves for books, installed screens and curtains, and were now building a water-sealed toilet, one of the only two toilets in the barrio. Screens and water tanks were unusual too (a large majority of volunteers had neither). Along with the books, medical kits, typewriters, and other extras, they made their simple thatched house seem like a special palace to the children who visited during the long noon break from school or who came after school to play, read, or just watch. Medical kits made some volunteers adjuncts to the local *herbolarios,* or rural health clinics. Bill had tended a deep bolo cut of a neighboring farmer. Other volunteers regularly cleaned infections, put ointment on burns, and a few even saved lives through a quick and ingenious use of their limited medical knowledge and their amply stocked kits.

The children noticed the special, strange foods that Ralph and Bill had brought back from the city after attending a workshop on science. The boys had made a pudding out of yesterday's rice and topped it with chocolate syrup and cinnamon. Last night they had had chicken and some of the children were envious. To the Filipino children, the fact that the volunteers could afford chicken and that their houses—modest as they were, and there were no more modest homes anywhere in the Peace Corps—were filled with such things as medical kits, books, and magazines was proof that America was almost as fabulously rich as they had imagined.

Volunteers contended with snakes, scorpions, lizards, and rats just as their Filipino neighbors did. They inhaled the same smell of the nearby garbage pit. They usually ate nothing more than rice and fish or rice and local vegetables or a piece of pork, and had chicken or beef only when it was available. But they were *americanos,* with special status, privileges, and things. They knew it and so did their Filipino hosts.

Tonight there was to be a feast in the barrio celebrating the marriage of the daughter of the barrio lieutenant. Bill and Ralph would try again *kari-kari* (stewed pigs' intestines), *balut* (nearly hatched ducks' eggs), squid stewed in its own ink, fishhead and fishhead soup (with eyeballs afloat) as well as the usual rice or *pancit* (fried noodles). For Filipinos, there was no better way to show love for volunteers than to invite them to a party, which usually meant dancing, eating, and singing. Some volunteers recorded heroic dancing and eating feats, knowing that to refuse a dance or food would offend the hospitable friends who might not understand why the lovely *americana* could not dance the twist for hours on end or the handsome *americano* could not digest dog meat or spiced pig entrails.

Usually at night Ralph and Bill talked quietly in their *sala* (small parlor), played checkers, read a book, or prepared the lesson. Sometimes there was a program at the school or the town plaza, but most days and nights were quiet and passed one into the other. As babies were born and young and old died, as the tides came and receded, and the rainy and dry seasons interchanged with each other, the steady rhythm of barrio life and death was rarely interrupted.

Occasionally a volunteer's quiet day would be marked by an unpleasant incident: a mentally ill man following a girl for a mile down the road before she reached home safely; a *tuba*-filled politician attempting to involve a volunteer in a local political fight; a sudden, vicious whirling typhoon that flattened houses and destroyed the rice crop.

There were pleasurable dramas too: the rescue of a sinking fishing boat; saving a boy's life through mouth-to-mouth resuscitation; massaging the abdomen of a woman in labor because barrio neighbors believed it would make for an easy birth; or delivering the infant boy without difficulty. These and many other dramas like them were experienced by volunteers in the Philippines; but life did not often seem exciting. Pleasures were usually quite simple: a ribboned sunset; the deep brown eyes of a laughing youngster; a teacher asking for help. These were the comforts of volunteers as they faced the routine and often tiresome days and nights of life in the barrio.

BARRIO SCHOOLS AND THE VOLUNTEERS

In a poorer barrio in the eastern Visayas, Ralph's friend, Len, watched the windswept rain spray through his screenless *sala* window as night came. This day—the second day of classes following Christmas vacation—had gone like so many before it. Rain and wind. Inefficiency and delay. Len rested his chin in the cups of both hands, elbows on knees, and stared at the unchanging, wet, black outside.

Theoretically, classes had begun in June, but teachers were still being transferred in and out of school by August. In September word was passed by the head teacher that officials from the division office would make a visit toward the end of the month. For three weeks students spent much of their time hauling dirt, planting flowers, and building fences to prepare for the visit. Instruction seemed to be at a standstill.

October began hopefully. On the first few sunshiny days, classes started on time. All four teachers seemed enthusiastic. Then with high winds and drenching rain, absences were frequent. Teachers were called to the *población* for conferences and demonstration classes. On Monday mornings, school rarely began before nine thirty.

In November preparations began for the local, district, and provincial athletic meets. Some of the older students were sent to the central school for training, and during the last week of November school was officially dismissed so that all students could either participate in or attend the district meet.

Len shifted his gaze to the flickering light of two candles on his kitchen table. Glancing beyond the table, he saw a stick of mosquito repellent in an open medical kit. It won't do much good, he thought. While in the kitchen, he boiled water for coffee and rubbed the stick of repellent on his ankles, neck, arms, and around the belt line of his torso. Returning to his seat in the *sala*, he set the coffee on a small hardwood stool next to a lighted candle he had taken from the kitchen. Len gazed again at the pelting rain which had already turned the street outside to mud; he sipped his coffee and mused about the month just past.

December had been a month of parties. Immediately after the athletic meet, frenzied preparations began for the barrio fiesta on December 8. A week later classes were dismissed for the provincial athletic meet. Then came the pageantry and excitement of Christmas and many *meriendas*.

The vacation was over now, but classes were still not organized. Len arrived at school at 7:30 that morning. With another teacher and two students, they swept goat droppings out of the classroom. By eight o'clock—half an hour after classes were scheduled to begin—the fourth teacher arrived. Together, the teachers repaired the bamboo flagpole which had been blown over by increasingly strong winds coming off the ocean from the southeast. By nine o'clock classes were under way for the approximately 50 students who had come to school out of an enrollment of 150. Until 10:15, Len assisted in the sixth-grade class and made plans with the teacher to demonstrate artificial respiration on the following day. Later he visited other classes where teachers were filling out reports while students talked and laughed. Then the rains fell from the sky to drown his hopes for more effective teaching and higher attendance in the afternoon.

The rains continued, and Len shifted his gaze to the sputtering candlelight, and wondered if things would ever change. Would they change tomorrow, or next month, or next year? They wouldn't change tomorrow, for it was raining too hard now. Nor would they change this month or next, because it was the height of the rice harvesting season and many children would be needed to help with the harvest. In March teachers and children would be preoccupied with exams, filling out final forms and records, and with graduation. And next year, why would it be any different? Len put down his coffee cup, sat up, snuffed out the candle, and went to bed.

Across the road, the sixth-grade teacher, Mr. Abueva, was also about to go to sleep. Sitting in a hardwood chair, dressed only in his underwear, he puffed distractedly on an American cigarette. That Peace Corps boy was a puzzle, he thought. Always in a hurry; even when he eats, he hurries. Sometimes he is finished eating when we are just beginning. When he rests, he doesn't seem to rest. He is always filling in the time, reading a book, building equipment, fixing something. He is so nervous. Perhaps he does not yet feel at home with us. Tomorrow we must have a friendly chat.

Mr. Abueva crushed his cigarette stub, and called his son for a bottle of San Miguel beer. The trouble is, he thought, whenever I chat with that Peace Corps boy, he is always criticizing. First, he said we spent too much time on ground improvement. But he was wrong. The Division Superintendent was pleased with our grounds. Then, Len did not like the athletic meets. But we won in the district and we would have won in the province if we had been better prepared. This morning he was angry because many students stayed home. But who can stop the rain? Not me. Not him either. *Bahala na* (never mind), tomorrow we will have a chat. I will have Martina make him a rice cake.

The San Miguel tasted good. It tingled on Mr. Abueva's tongue and throat. Len likes rice cakes, the teacher reflected, and he likes San Miguel too. He's a good boy, my Peace Corps volunteer. What if he chooses to live next door to a cemetery? The Americans don't believe in ghosts. Maybe they don't have them in America. He is a good boy, anyway. Could we have repaired the flagpole without him this morning? And didn't he stop the leak in the roof of the fourth-grade classroom? He's a good boy, but strange. Always in a hurry. *Bahala na.* Americans are like that.

EDUCATIONAL AIDES

Mr. Abueva and Len had two completely different views of education (to Mr. Abueva, it was to teach children what was right and wrong; to Len, it was to liberate the mind). They had different views of the school system (to Mr. Abueva, the school bureaucracy was something one became accustomed to; to Len, it was something to be changed). They even had different ideas about Len's role in the Peace Corps in the Philippines (Len thought he had come to do a job; Mr. Abueva wanted more than anything that Len should enjoy himself). Because the volunteers had come to the Philippines under the assumption that they were needed to do an important job of teaching English and science, they were totally unprepared to find that most of them were trained for "non-jobs." I recall my own dismay at hearing the first explanation of the volunteer's job by an official of the Philippine Bureau of Public Schools. He was an old and wise man who had served the public schools of the Philippines for more than forty years, first as a teacher, then as a principal and superintendent, and finally, on the eve of his retirement, as an administrator in the ramshackle, overcrowded building which housed the Department of Education in Manila. Only a few days before the arrival of the first group of volunteers, he explained the non-job of an educational aide to a group of Filipino newsmen at a press conference: "If a teacher asks a volunteer to speak a sentence with correct English pronunciation, the educational aide will oblige the teacher." A reporter pressed him, "But surely that isn't all these Americans can do?" The old school official squinted his eyes, deepening the creases which radiated toward his temples, and after a long period of quiet remarked, "They can help in other ways. They can hold up maps." Then as an afterthought, "Americans are great gadgeteers. They know science. The volunteers can build science equipment and begin science clubs."

The old school official was vague because he knew little more than anyone else what the new and diffuse role of educational aide (created especially for the volunteers) would be. Many barrio parents, in awe of *americanos*, would have had no hesitation in turning over complete responsibility for school administration and teaching to the young newcomers, but wiser, more cautious heads in Manila preferred either a vague or limited description of the responsibilities of volunteers. Top officials at the Bureau of Public Schools were saying, "We are pleased to have the help of young Americans but we will have to see how well they fit into a vast, ongoing political and administrative structure before we say too much about just what their role will be."

EDUCATION IN THE PHILIPPINES

The Philippine school system had been founded by Americans in the colonial period. Thousands of wood and nipa schoolhouses were built and well over one thousand American instructors, including the Thomasites, came to teach English and the democratic way of life. Under the Spanish, Filipinos had been made to go to church. Under the Americans, they were obliged to attend school. Public elementary and high school enrollment jumped from about 150,000 in 1900 to more than 1 million in 1921, over 2 million in 1940, and to more than 6 million at the time of the arrival of Peace Corps volunteers in October, 1961.

By 1961 the schools in the Philippines constituted the most important social, economic, and political institutions in the country. For several years approximately one third of the national budget had been earmarked for education. To Filipino congressmen, the educational budget meant an opportunity to bargain with the Secretary of Education over appointments and school construction in exchange for votes on educational matters. Even the appointment of janitors could be a matter of political interest. A janitor in a *población* school, who earned about 60 pesos a month and received his check regularly, was considerably richer than most of his neighbors who were lucky to average an income of a peso a day, depending upon the planting and harvesting season. (Four pesos could be exchanged for approximately one dollar.) The beginning teacher, after completing a two-year normal curriculum, earned 1,800 pesos a year, and a four-year normal school graduate received a salary of 2,100 pesos, a high salary in the barrio or even in a *población*.

Teaching meant money; it also meant security. The regular teacher—about three fourths of all public elementary schoolteachers were regulars when the volunteers arrived—acquires lifetime tenure after passing a civil service examination. Perhaps even more than income and security, teachers valued the prestige assigned to them by the people in the barrios. During the Spanish rule, education had been for the elite only. It was intended to enforce and perpetuate social distinctions, a concept that had burrowed deeply into the Filipino consciousness and remained even after the Americans had proclaimed the idea of education for all. Today education remains the key to social position as well as political and economic opportunity in the Philippines.

To adminster a public school system which provides teachers for more than 4 million public elementary students in 18,000 barrios, over 1,000 municipalities, and 35 cities of the 56 provinces of the Philippines there exists an elaborate administrative hierarchy. The administration of the Bureau of Public Schools is led by a Director and twenty-two top Manila officials. For every province and thirteen cities there is a Division Superintendent who leads an army of Assistant Superintendents, Division (provincial) Supervisors, District Superintendents and Supervisors (districts are subdivisions of provinces), and their clerical staffs.

The Director, usually a career man chosen by the Secretary of Education—a presidential appointee—is given power under the law to establish primary schools, fix salaries within the limits set by the law, organize curricula, prescribe the authority of principals, and approve plans for the construction of schools. Theoretically, the vast bureaucracy is run in minute detail from the general office in Manila, which sends circulars, memorandums, and general letters in profusion to lesser officials in the provinces. Actually, the power of Division Superintendents can be great. Under authority delegated from the Director, they appoint municipal schoolteachers and have control over the use of provincial and municipal school buildings. More important, they may have strong support from the local politicians or even congressmen. In some provinces Division Superintendents and even District Supervisors run their schools as personal dukedoms or baronies.

The runaway birth rate of the Philippines means a burgeoning school population each year and more power for the Division Superintendent who must request new classes and pass on new teachers. Any prospective new teacher interviewed by the Division Superintendent would have graduated from one of nine public normal colleges or from a private college offering a normal school curriculum, and would have passed the teacher's selection examination. Almost all beginning teachers are assigned to newly created classes called "extension classes" to handle the annual increases in enrollment. The Secretary of Education requests Congress to authorize extension classes for approximately every forty additional students enrolled in each grade, but Congress usually appropriates money for only about half the number requested, and these invariably are allocated by the Secretary in school divisions identified with the most powerful members of the majority party in Congress. Superintendents in these divisions then distribute classes on the basis of need and political or personal choice. In addition to new teachers, there are additional principals appointed to schools which become full elementary (all six grades) rather than primary (first four grades). Some teachers succeed in being transferred closer to their homes or *poblaciones* or to a desired central school or to the city (if that is their choice). Other teachers, incurring the disfavor of a powerful principal or someone in the division office—perhaps the Superintendent himself—are sentenced to less desirable posts.

In addition to constituting an important political and economic institution, the school is the main organized carrier and inculcator of Filipino values. If the school system is hierarchical, authoritarian, personalized, family-centered, and fatalistic, it is because these are major features of Filipino culture. The emphasis on hierarchy and authority pervades the schools. A visit to a barrio school by division officials sends principal and teachers into a frenzy of preparation for days. The grounds must be cleared, the stones and fence painted, and a feast prepared. Similar harried preparations take place on a larger scale at a central school when visitors from the general office in Manila descend on it.

THE FILIPINO RECEPTION

At first, few volunteers realized the extent to which their problems with the non-job of educational aide reflected deep-seated cultural differences between Americans and Filipinos. "What kind of a job is this, anyway," asked many volunteers. They could not replace teachers. There were an endless number of possibilities as to how they could spend their time—teach various units in cooperation with the teacher, work with remedial or enrichment groups, assist in demonstration teaching, help organize extracurricular activities, construct science equipment and visual aids, work with the guides for teaching English as a second language—but it was not clear what was wanted and why.

Volunteers would ask teachers and principals, "What do you want me to do?" Principals and teachers, raising eyebrows to express sympathy for the volunteers, would respond, "What do you want to do?" More than anything, most of them wanted to work; but at what? The role of educational aide was nothing and everything at the same time.

Thousands of Filipinos were intrigued at the thought of having a personal representative of President Kennedy living down the road in a bamboo and nipa-thatched house. They were puzzled that Americans should want to live so simply. They were perplexed when these Americans said they came to work in the schools under the direction of Filipinos. They were confused when the volunteers reported that they were not teachers but merely educational aides. Other Americans had come to the Philippines as administrators, teachers, supervisors, and soldiers. They always seemed to take charge. They knew what to do. They accepted the benefits which went with high status and authority. Puzzled teachers and barrio neighbors sometimes speculated that perhaps the real mission of the volunteers was to report on Communists (practically none existed except in central Luzon). Principals and District Supervisors, aware that the volunteers assigned to them lacked a thorough training in teaching methods, often assumed that they were merely ambassadors of goodwill. That was the most comfortable assumption for everyone to make about the newcomers. Filipinos knew what to do with ambassadors of goodwill. Show them a good time; make them comfortable and happy. But what does one do with an educational aide? An assistant teacher? A coteacher? A demonstration teacher?

As ambassadors of goodwill, status symbols, and potential donors of material goods, volunteers were welcomed by division and district officials and principals and head teachers. Even at the highest educational levels in Manila, Filipino officials continued to think of volunteers mainly as ambassadors of goodwill for about a year after the first volunteers had reached the field. When I asked the Secretary of Education to evaluate the work of volunteers in August, 1962, he replied that they were doing wonderfully because they ate the food of Filipinos, danced their dances, and tried to learn their languages. The Director of the Bureau of Public Schools responded to my urging for a critique of the performance of volunteers by pointing out that some of the girls were too independent in their dress and behavior, and that some volunteers had bypassed their principals or supervisors in making complaints directly to higher officials. He said nothing of English, science, or mathematics. The Director—like the Superintendents and Supervisors in the field—seemed much more interested in whether or not the volunteers were enjoying themselves and making others happy than if they knew how to use the guides for teaching English as a second language which had been developed by his own Bureau of Public Schools and AID.

In this respect Filipino officials—while exemplifying their own culture—were also in agreement with certain policy tendencies in the Peace Corps itself. Statements from Washington and Manila repeatedly emphasized that Peace Corps programs did not constitute technical assistance. The Peace Corps, Filipino hosts were informed by some visitors from Washington and by myself, while anxious to promote more effective teaching of English and science in the schools, was interested primarily in creating human relationships based on mutual respect and understanding.

ACHIEVEMENT VERSUS BAHALA NA

For a while most volunteers accepted the necessity for simply observing classes, and many of them sat in the back of the room for several months. "We were told to help the teachers," wrote a volunteer, "but the help part was up to us . . . workshops, conferences, special classes, demonstration classes, group projects, community projects. . . . There were periods of extreme boredom when I had to search for a new approach or idea, anything to keep busy. . . . Let us teach, plant rice, build roads, but give us some definite work to do!"

More than anything else, volunteers wanted to succeed in doing something significant. They had an overriding desire to meet some real need and use their influence in a tangible way. For many of the younger volunteers, this was the first chance to do something on their own. As one of them put it, "The Peace Corps for me is the first major step into the world." Another girl wrote, "I had the feeling that my mettle had never been tested." Work was an incontestable virtue to most volunteers. Like Emerson, they found success in work to be "hat and coat, food and wine . . . health and holiday."

It is not the passion for work or workmanship which distinguishes Americans. Germans (particularly Protestants), Swiss, and Scandinavians frequently complain that Americans are lackadaisical and careless in their work. The American passion has been for achievement in work to prove the worth of the individual, something which is not guaranteed by caste, class, family name or position, or responsibility within the family in middle-class America. The American drive has been to test one's mettle.

The Peace Corps telegram which announced that the volunteer had been accepted for training usually stimulated an excited feeling of potential significance, but training in the United States was largely sedentary and academic. For many, it was ten weeks of marking time. As one of them wrote, "There remained a silent resolute feeling that once out in the barrio, away from all the training, we would be on our own, self-sufficient, and able to begin to move." Then came the reality of *bahala na* in the barrios.

The deepest meaning of *bahala na* (it doesn't matter, never mind) is that the conditions of life are unchanging and unchangeable. To American volunteers, restlessly anx-

ious to improve the world, almost everything mattered
desperately, at least at first. They were confounded repeatedly by the Filipino sense of time. As one of them
wrote about his fellow teachers, "To them, now means
sometime before tomorrow." The rules of the school system
often reflected American ideas about punctuality, but the
behavior of teachers and students was governed by *bahala
na.* The rule stating that teachers and other school employees were expected to be in their respective rooms at
least five minutes before the beginning of each session was
frequently ignored, and many volunteers tried to persuade
their fellow teachers to start and close classes on time.

Most volunteers sooner or later adjusted to Filipino
standards of punctuality. It was much more difficult to accept the pervasive underlying fatalism which made the introduction of new ideas and methods in Filipino life so
difficult. Since Filipinos denounced disease, illiteracy, low
agricultural production, and poverty, and ritualistically advertised their admiration for American standards of living,
it was sometimes difficult to understand their deep resistance to change. A girl on the island of Masbate wrote of
her early months, "I wanted to help in so many ways but I
could not because the people would not let me. . . .They
were not interested in what I had to say or do [or in] any
improvement or new idea which would involve change."
Her feelings of frustration were extreme, but others felt
comparable resistance.

Most upsetting of all, from the point of view of the volunteers, was that the means to better education, food, and
health were at hand. It was only a matter of will. It was a
question of implementing the rhetoric of Filipino politicians and school superintendents with action. Most volunteers believed that if Filipinos really wanted to change life
for the better—more efficient, productive, and healthful—
they could.

In the early months inefficiency in Filipino organization
was a source of considerable tension for volunteers. One

girl wrote from Panay, "I have spent hours just sitting in a truck, waiting for it to go; usually I bring a book or engage in a conversation to help me forget the time, but I still think over and over how not only my time is being wasted, but everyone else's too." Eventually most volunteers perceived that while Filipinos were inefficient by American standards, they were remarkably successful at getting things to work their way. Truck drivers could dismantle engines and transmissions in the middle of the road surrounded by cackling chickens and snorting pigs and put transmission parts together with rubber bands and tape. Filipinos accomplished things in their own way, and in their own time. But—and this was the rub—volunteers often wanted them to do things another way and more quickly.

To the extent that *bahala na* meant a fundamental acceptance of the basic conditions of life and death, most volunteers resisted it to the end. To the extent that it de-emphasized the American emphasis on the "vital importance" of a myriad of decisions and actions which, from a new perspective, no longer seemed vitally important, many volunteers eventually felt *bahala na* became a part of their own personalities. *Bahala na* could be a helpful response to the minor annoyances of daily life—a missed bus, no fish in the market, a sudden storm—but it also appeared to be a chief obstacle to progress in health, education, and economic development.

Bahala na in the face of unnecessary death (from the volunteer's view) was profoundly discouraging. One of them, returning from the funeral of a small child, wrote that he died not from some incurable disease, but because "the woman who dutifully lit the twisted candles felt no personal responsibility when she saw her baby coughing and crying." He went on, "I can pity the mother's lack of education, and work all the harder to see that the next generation doesn't have to repeat the scene quite as often. But this picture is repeated all over now . . . sometimes the mourners are dressed in fine black *piña* and expensive *barongs.* Sometimes they are teachers or engineers . . . more education for what?"

Volunteers discovered that in the barrios most Filipinos believed that the world behaves according to unknown and unknowable forces. Those often appear in the form of supernatural beings who control life and death, sickness and health, pregnancy and infertility. The acceptance of Roman Catholicism under the Spanish regime did not destroy earlier beliefs in evil spirits and ancient taboos and sacrifices to ward against them. For millions of Filipinos, the Christian God and traditional gods existed side by side. Catholic saints and pre-Christian spirits in the form of familiar animals or exotic, weird beings must be appeased equally. Both the priest and the shaman must be obeyed; and the rural health doctor and the *herbolario* followed.

While hunting rats in the attic of his house on Samar, one volunteer came upon a strange-looking collection of dried leaves hanging from the ceiling. As he began to remove the leaves, his houseboy became violently excited and shouted, "Stop! It protects the house from danger!" This particular concoction was an antidote against a specific evil spirit.

The lives of the children taught by volunteers were filled with warnings about various witches and spirits to be assuaged or avoided. The most common was the *aswang,* a human being who changes himself into either a flying *aswang* who sucks blood from the sick and dying and from the fetuses of pregnant women, or the *aswang* who appears on the ground in another animal or human form to scare and confuse people, dig up corpses, or wait for the sick to die to eat their liver. Volunteers encountered reports of more than a dozen similar spirits, ghosts, or giants, and discovered that they played a vital part in the lives of their neighbors, children, and teachers.

Although generally intolerant of what they regarded as superstitions, many volunteers were especially upset by those Filipino beliefs which seemed to block progress to-

ward better health and life. In some barrios, neither mother
nor newborn infant was permitted to take a bath for a period of from twenty to thirty days in order to appease the
aswang. Since in some places illness is attributed to the
spirits or to the *mangkukulam*, a person believed to be a
sorcerer, who practices magic through a doll, a chicken, or
even a look, medical practices urged by volunteers seemed
irrelevant to many Filipinos. One volunteer, after persuad-
ing a Filipino to help finance a harelip operation for one of
his students, was prevented by the child's grandfather from
taking her to the hospital because, as he put it, "Harelips
bring the family good luck." The little girl had been happy
about the planned operation; the parents were cooperative;
the volunteer was hopeful that the operation would be a
success. But the grandfather and his particular superstition
prevented it. Volunteers found it hard to shrug their shoul-
ders and say, "*Bahala na*."

THE CRAVING FOR WORK

Education was the task of the Peace Corps in the Philippines but educational aides, determined, energetic, and
zealous for results, struggled to find satisfaction in the non-
job. Where was the rising level of expectations which volunteers had read about in the American newspapers?
Where were the Filipinos who would say and mean, "We
need what you have to give"? It usually took some time before volunteers could locate them. In the meantime, they
were driven by the desire to help in the ways for which
their own culture had prepared them. "It is painfully obvious to me," wrote one boy, "that no matter how well you
were trained, no matter how good your intentions, if you
can't find an adequate way to give your contribution, then
you'll be heading for inside the big whale's belly." Another
volunteer, a girl, wrote sadly, "We seem to have such a
tremendous need to pay our way."

Nearly a year after he had arrived in his barrio, one boy wrote home to a friend, "The big question every volunteer asks is whether or not he is accomplishing anything." "I am happiest when I am actively busy," wrote a girl from a southern state, commenting, "I thoroughly enjoy hard, challenging work that keeps me active from morning to evening." But ceaseless activity in a *bahala na* culture did not often result in tangible accomplishment. She often felt "as if I were just batting my head against a brick wall." Another volunteer, a girl from New York City, complained, "Just to be put in a place to smile, be there, and satisfy the status-striving of some superintendent is not sufficient justification for our being here. . . . I would rather be overworked and exhausted from a hard day's work than underemployed and exhausted from having nothing to do all day because no one is really interested in what I want to do."

Eventually most volunteers would learn that through patience and deep listening, but not necessarily through ceaseless activity, they could help themselves as well as Filipinos to learn, change, and grow. Hard work, many would discover, did not necessarily mean constant motion. But the lesson was to be a difficult one. The feeling that activity for its own sake is good is a common American feeling that is not easily dispelled. I recall a visit to a small community in the Bicol region of Luzon approximately three or four months after the first group of volunteers had arrived in the Philippines. I found about a dozen volunteers had gathered from distant communities to spend a weekend building a stone wall around a school. The volunteers disapproved of the emphasis given to stone walls in the Philippines. They longed to reach the minds of the children and teachers with whom they worked. They wished that less Filipino money and time went into building walls and school beautification campaigns, but they were joyously happy from the sheer release of human energy in building that wall. Many months later some of the same volunteers, responding to President Kennedy's emphasis on physical fitness for the nation, went on a fifty-mile hike to gain the same releasing effect.

DEFINING THE NON-JOB

The vague non-job of educational aide seemed to many volunteers to be a particularly perverse expression of the *bahala na* culture. Some of them, a minority in the earliest groups and probably a majority later, found ways to define the job in school which were reasonably satisfying. Those who had teaching experience or training back home often were quickest to leave their roles as observers in the back of the classroom and develop specific in-school projects. Some demonstrated new teaching techniques in regular classes, or presented them after class to groups of teachers. Others did "team teaching" (sharing a class with the regular teacher). They worked with a few teachers who were especially interested in learning the new English guides. Some volunteers assisted with lesson plans in science for units which were unfamiliar to the regular teachers, or built simple science equipment or took children on field trips. Especially talented volunteers taught classes in music, art, journalism, current events, or physical education. Others developed curriculum guides, in-service training programs, and library programs. They wrote and directed children's plays, planned a Christmas program, and drilled children in preparation for the athletic meets.[1]

The ability of volunteers to find satisfying in-school work depended to a considerable extent on their principals, head teachers, and teachers. Where, as on the small island off the coast of Panay there was a shortage of teachers, a boy was put in front of the classroom to take charge soon after he arrived. For him there was no problem of the non-job. One girl on the island of Negros developed team-teaching arrangements in the third, fourth, fifth, and sixth

[1] *See Chapter 5 on the several stages of coping with the non-job.*

grades within a few weeks after her arrival. In rare situations highly motivated teachers, spotting a particular talent or skill in a volunteer, requested specific assistance. A boy in Cebu held a series of daily hour-long seminars with his teachers after school in addition to spending a half hour each day with fourth-, fifth-, and sixth-grade classes. Soon teachers in Cebu City asked him to conduct a weekly series of seminars in English and science on Saturdays, and nearly a third of the eligible teachers of the city attended. Such occurrences were more frequent with volunteers in the later groups, particularly groups eight and nine, more than a year and a half after the Peace Corps first arrived in the Philippines.

In the earlier months, volunteers with a clear conception of their in-school objectives were as rare as highly motivated Filipino teachers with a clear notion of how to use volunteers. Teachers and volunteers constantly perplexed each other. Some teachers seemed obviously pleased with the presence of young Americans, and would have been willing to have them take over responsibility for classes. A minority of teachers seemed to resent the youth and frankness of the volunteers. Some suspected that they were representatives of the Bureau of Public Schools. A great many resisted the introduction of a new method of teaching English as a second language. Large numbers were reluctant to spend extra time needed to improve their lesson plans.

VOLUNTEERS AND TEACHERS

The most common reception given by teachers was a mixture of friendship, curiosity, deference, shyness, apprehension, and understanding. They were usually anxious to please and said what they thought volunteers wanted to hear rather than what they themselves felt. Even when they were apprehensive or suspicious, teachers wanted the volunteers to be comfortable. It was later discovered that many teachers were disappointed in the volunteers' seeming lack of training in methods and subject matter, but they usually did not show it to the representatives of President Kennedy's rich and powerful country. Their feelings of inferiority as Filipinos in relationship to Americans, because of the relative wealth and power of the two countries, was compounded by their fear of being ashamed by making mistakes in English or by exposing their ignorance of science. Sometimes their shyness may have been mistaken for apathy by the volunteers who were discouraged when teachers failed to take advantage of proffered help. But apathy existed, as it does in any large school system or bureaucracy. Teachers frequently complained to volunteers about bad curricula, corrupt supervisors, overcentralization, or the lack of funds, but unlike their American listeners, they would not take the initiative to change things. To the volunteers, looking through American cultural lenses, they often seemed apathetic and even hypocritical.

After a while the most sensitive volunteers began to put themselves in the teacher's place. They began to realize, as one of them put it, "with a sinking spirit . . . how they must view me as a friendly eccentric who could afford to indulge in creativity and openness to new experiences since I didn't have the responsibilities they did; nor did I have to answer to superintendents or supervisors." Volunteers wondered how they would like it if a foreigner came into their class to show them how to teach something, especially if the foreigner was really quite inadequate in training and experience as a teacher. "I got the feeling that I was trespassing," wrote a girl from the Bicol, "even though the teachers would stop whatever they were doing to let me have the class in English."

The apathy of the teachers and their acceptance of authoritarianism and exploitation in the school system even became understandable when one felt the massive power of the system and the isolation and the loneliness of the teacher. A volunteer from Negros wrote of the teacher in a "faraway little primary school where she teaches a combination class (grades two and three at the same time) and has her own four little preschoolers under her feet because she has no baby-sitter. No one has visited her in a long time; not even the District Supervisor cares what she does." With such empathy many volunteers developed warm, supportive friendships with their coteachers which led to deep, rich mutual growth.

WHAT AM I DOING HERE?

Many volunteers—even those who made close friendships with teachers—reacted to the frustrations of the non-job by wondering if the Peace Corps was fulfilling a useful purpose in the Philippines. Those without teaching experience found themselves asking: "Am I competent? What do I know about child development? Dare I make a suggestion? Do I want to work with elementary school children? What will this have to do with my career when I leave the Peace Corps?" A large majority of the volunteers had no experience in working in any large bureaucracy before. Many had just graduated from college. Others had interrupted their graduate education. Another group had held one or more jobs for only a year or two. They had no experience against which to judge the slow-moving Filipino school system, lethargic children, indifferent and nonintellectual teachers who did not share their interests. They had no experience with educational decisions which were politically inspired and the inefficiency of highly centralized bureaucracies. They did not realize that the same problems, although perhaps not in the same degree, would obtain in many school systems in the United States.[2]

Some volunteers who could not find satisfaction in school became convinced that they should not be trying to teach English at all. They asked, "Why teach English to third-graders, a majority of whom will never graduate sixth

---

[2] *Ex-volunteers now report being appalled by politics, bureaucracy, and selfishness in American school systems.*

grade and rarely use English in their adult lives in the barrio?" "Why teach English to sixth-graders when at some high schools the dialect is used as the language of instruction?" "Why teach English when classroom space is so frequently crowded that two classes are grouped in a room meant for one with three or four students sharing a single desk and when textbooks are not always available?" "Why teach English when the stomachs of 95 percent of the children are full of worms, and children can't concentrate because of malnutrition?" "Why teach English as a second language with its emphasis on pattern drills which will enforce the habit of rote memorization?" "Why teach English when Filipinos should develop a national pride based on a national language of their own?" "Why, why, why . . . ?" There were answers to the whys. They all added up to the fact that without the spread of English, national, economic, and political development in the Philippines would be retarded severely. Despite the answers, some volunteers remained convinced that education was the wrong field for Peace Corps service in the Philippines.

ESCAPE FROM THE NON-JOB

One way to escape the non-job was to find a principal who would let a volunteer take over a class by himself. Since this was forbidden by the Bureau of Public Schools in the elementary schools, a few volunteers received permission to be reassigned to high schools where they could have control over a class. Some were ingenious in finding situations almost anywhere outside the elementary schools. A boy in the Bicol taught journalism once a week to a high school class, current events to three sections of seniors of another high school, adult reading classes in his barrio twice a week, and English and science one night a week in a folk school near the barrio. These jobs were his answer to aimless wandering on the non-job.

The range of volunteer community activity was extraordinary. Building libraries and toilets were the most common projects. Dozens of campaigns were begun and many of them concluded with varying degrees of success. In one library on a small island off the coast of Samar there was a large daily turnover of books and almost eight hundred were borrowed in the first year. The municipal council hired a librarian to continue after the departure of the volunteer who sparked the library. Other libraries, begun with much fanfare, including speeches and fiestas, rapidly fell into disuse.

Several volunteers studied books and pamphlets on agriculture, and many began model gardens. A boy in Cebu introduced a variety of tomato which was resistant to blight and wilt. He began informal discussions on agriculture with students in the afternoons, and after a while farmers stopped at his house for information or to buy seedlings. Several volunteers grew rice in an attempt to introduce the newest and best techniques (fertilizer, insecticide, pesticide, and improved seed) and one girl on Catanduanes actually was given a small plot of land, a carabao, and seedlings by a friendly Filipino to help her start a small farm.

Piggery and poultry projects were also common. An enterprising volunteer helped the vice-mayor of his municipality begin a poultry business. The boy raised baby chicks past the dangerous stage and sold them at cost to the official. In this way he eventually introduced one thousand chickens in his town through a group of seven Filipinos. The oldest volunteer in the first four groups (he was in his fifties, and he and his wife were the only volunteers in the first four groups over thirty) expressed a strong interest in building compost piles to the science supervisor of his division. With the cooperation of the schools and the mayor in his municipality, he conducted a science demonstration for science teachers, farmers, and community development personnel. As a result, six other communities requested demonstrations.

At least as many volunteers became involved in health projects as in farming. A successful toilet campaign was carried out on a small island off the coast of Panay. In many other cases toilets were built to please volunteers or to be displayed as status symbols, but they were hardly used at all. One boy tried a wooden slipper campaign to attempt to cut down on illness caused by worms. Others—especially in groups three and four—helped several children to obtain operations to remove harelips. On the island of Masbate, a determined volunteer coordinated a cholera inoculation campaign with mixed success. One girl in the Bicol spent every Thursday teaching art and English at a leprosarium.

A few volunteers reacted to the non-job by becoming one-man aid programs contrary to Peace Corps intent. They arranged with schools in the United States to send books to the Philippines, to establish revolving loan funds or scholarship funds for students, or purchase chemistry reagents or equipment for science classes. They did not want to play Santa Claus, but they could not resist the temptation to help individuals whom they liked and who were in need, especially if they were uncertain as to whether they were helping them in the non-job at school.

The first summer vacation from school in May and June provided volunteers from groups one and two with the opportunity to plunge into a variety of out-of-school jobs. Several gained a new satisfaction teaching classes on their own at normal schools and high schools. Others even organized and administered schools. One group of girls teamed with Filipina nurses, and visited barrios—which had never been visited by a rural health doctor—to run treatment clinics and first-aid, nutrition, and public sanitation seminars. A group of twelve volunteers organized and supervised educational-recreational facilities at Welfareville in Mandaluyong, Luzon, where more than eighteen thousand children—orphans, mental defectives, delinquents, and mentally ill—were housed. Many volunteers organized summer camps in their communities. Camp Brotherhood, on the island of Negros, was organized and administered by volunteers but funded by well-to-do Filipinos to give several hundred poor malnourished children an opportunity for a summer learning experience.

Dozens of volunteers rushed to their summer projects from the non-job with a sense of exhilaration. Wrote a girl from the Bicol who worked from early morning to midnight to run her summer camp, "My spirits were lifted one hundred per cent by the sheer releasing force of work. For the first time since I had arrived, I had a real job to do—a challenge—and the effect of this on my well-being cannot be overstressed." A volunteer at Camp Brotherhood wrote that his job at camp "accounted for two months of the hardest work I have ever done, and I can say the most enjoyable time I have ever had." Months later another boy, looking back on his reasons for helping to organize the camp, acknowledged that he hoped it would bring him a personal sense of achievement and recognition as compared to the "seemingly intangible and unrewarded role of remaining in the barrio and attempting to work with the minds of children."

THE NON-JOB IS EVERYWHERE

Returning to their communities at the conclusion of the summer vacation, volunteers continued to cope with the problems of the non-job. Increasingly, they recognized that their problems were due not just to the lack of role definition or the absence of teaching objectives and skills, but to deeper forces inherent in the conflicts between *americano* ways of doing and thinking and Filipino culture. Apathy, delay, and inefficiency had been present in most summer projects too, and it thwarted many ambitious community development plans in health and agriculture. The boy who began the wooden slipper campaign in a flush of enthusiasm found that after he left the barrio for a week, 95 percent of his *bakya* converts had gone back to their barefoot ways. The cholera inoculation campaign on Masbate sputtered because many people were more interested in the color animation of the anticholera film than its message about sanitation and immunization. Volunteers who gave first-aid assistance were in competition with local *herbolarios,* whose cures included the use of leaves or dirt for cuts. Many farmers—giving lip service to the methods proposed by a volunteer—would find an excuse not to use them. "Yes, fertilizer increases production, but our fields are too muddy."

The overwhelming tendency of volunteers in the early months was to deprecate even their modest accomplishments. Typical was the case of a boy in Negros Oriental who held the enthralled attention of a half-dozen students in a science experiment but who complained to me immediately after its completion that he was getting nowhere because at least a dozen of his children had wandered or been distracted. It was extremely difficult to gain perspective. Volunteers wanted to see a noticeable improvement in the children's English, an increased job interest of teachers, and general conversion to the virtues of indoor plumbing and literacy.

Most volunteers learned that it was not necessarily easier to create a job out of school than in school in a non-job culture. Some—demonstrating extraordinary sensitivity, patience, and persistence—eventually helped to create community projects which had widespread acceptance in their areas: a library supported by twenty-one barrios, administered by a local youth club in each barrio; special arithmetic classes based on programmed material for 35 to 55 out-of-school youths in a barrio of 2,000 people; a folk school where 80 out-of-school youths who had no possibility of going to high school were taught English, science, and nutrition. But most volunteers continued to struggle with their assignment as educational aides in school.

While the non-job threw most of the volunteers for a loss at first, there were exceptions who relished it. A volunteer from group three, praising the concept of educational aide, wrote, "One must determine what one's goals are. In fact, one must determine what one's job is, how to create a desire among people, and to define the means and develop the self-discipline to accomplish the job. One is as free to create as one is able." Another volunteer said, "In no other job could you find the freedom to select the way in which you as an individual will be most beneficial to a group, and then to move in that direction as far and as fast as the group of people will let you." Others learned to love the freedom and flexibility of the educational aide role too, but the very flexibility which presented such a challenge also created anguish and frustration.

There were many nights when Len went to bed wondering why Filipinos, who lived in poverty and disease, seemed so disorganized, inefficient, lazy, and superstitious, while, across the street, Mr. Abueva, puffing on a cigarette, wondered why Len often seemed critical, aggressive, insensitive, and mechanical. Volunteers had come from a country whose people, probably more than any other in history, had made personal achievement the standard of a man's worth. They came to a culture whose people felt a pervasive sense of *bahala na*. As Peace Corps experience the world over would show, it was the American who was peculiar.

III
Do you
eat rice?

: Self-reliance has been praised in America in a hundred different ways: in the pontifical speeches of politicians; in the board rooms of business tycoons; from the pulpit and the schoolmistress' desk; by the Tom Sawyers and Huck Finns; in the yearning hearts of immigrant sons; and in the popular poetry in the second half of the nineteenth and early part of the twentieth centuries. For more than two hundred years belief in the value of personal independence has pervaded American philosophy, literature, art, and science, molded American political, economic, and religious institutions, and guided an ever-expanding middle class in the rearing of their young.

TO PROMOTE SELF-RELIANCE

Valuing self-reliance for themselves, most Peace Corps volunteers were imbued with a powerful desire to stimulate it in others. They very much wanted to help Filipinos but mainly for the purpose of promoting self-help, a concept they would learn had no meaning in any of the Filipino dialects. One married volunteer wrote that she was considering giving a gift to her young *lavandera* (laundress) to enable her to go to school. "But," she added, "we'll try to give her no hint of the possibility before the fact." Gifts were not to be misunderstood. They should entail no obligation if they were to serve as spurs to self-sufficiency.

With Jefferson, volunteers believed that it was sacred and undeniable that all men are created independent and equal. Wrote one, "I have tried to stimulate an appreciation of the basic worth of the individual." Said another, "My concept of education is based on a belief in and respect for the individual and individualism." Another said that he had a "belief in the immense intellectual capabilities of the child despite his environment." He believed "in the need to teach children to think independently, not to parrot the 'truths' revealed to him by his teachers." Another volunteer wrote that he tried to foster the belief in "the distinctly American trait of each man believing he is as good as the next man."

Volunteers believed that individualism would lead to self-confidence. As one of them wrote, "I am trying to make [Filipino children] feel that each of them should not only be proud of themselves as individuals, but proud of their country and interested and concerned about their future." Volunteers warmed to the idea of teaching science inductively as a way of encouraging individuality. A girl volunteer wrote that she was thrilled when one teacher permitted a child to discover the principle of magnetism by herself and when another teacher let the children discover for themselves how germs could spoil fish. It was not enough for their students to repeat an English sentence pattern-drill correctly. "Think" questions were desired, not "fact" questions. Volunteers constantly prodded teachers and students to think for themselves and to speak frankly and even daringly.

It soon became obvious that the concept of self-reliance, as Americans understand it, was almost entirely alien to Filipino culture. "All too often even the very young have symptoms of sickening resignation, born of the feeling that one lowly man can do nothing," said one boy. In traditional societies help is not something one does for oneself. Help is provided by superiors to subordinates who grant favors and yield loyalty in exchange. A few volunteers even began to wonder whether the Peace Corps, whose representatives were treated with deference by Filipinos as potential workers of magic and bearers of things, merely reinforced attitudes of inferiority. They were caught in the dilemma of trying to promote self-reliance by helping others in a culture which did not value individual initiative in the first place.

UTANG NA LOOB VERSUS INDEPENDENCE AND EQUALITY

Most barrio dwellers not only doubted their capacity to change their own lives, but they believed that the individual had meaning only as part of a cohesive group—usually the extended family—whose members were bound together in a complicated network of hierarchical roles and reciprocal obligations. Rather than valuing independence in relationships—freedom from restraint in the exercise of choice—they emphasized *utang na loob,* a complex reciprocity of gratitude and obligation which keeps the members of families and villages living in harmony with each other and helps to protect them from outside forces.[1]

[1] *Strictly speaking,* utang na loob *refers to a debt of gratitude which arises from asking for a favor. I use it here in its broadest implications since nearly all Filipino relationships are based on continuing reciprocal obligations.*

The pervasive American cult of individuality was matched against the nearly universal Filipino belief in dependence through relatives, *compadres,* or other sponsors. The American belief in equality of opportunity was set against the overwhelming Filipino acceptance of a fixed (not earned) hierarchy of statuses and privileges.

For some volunteers individualism and equalitarianism became a moral crusade. One girl wrote, "I've tried to be an example of the American way of life, showing them the dignity of working with one's hands, thinking for oneself, being helpful to others . . . not because one is obligated to do so." On another island a married volunteer tried to inculcate the ideal of equality into two high school students who lived in her home. Although they helped with the chores, she would not call them servants. "Their position is as members rather than servants in our household. . . . We ask their ideas and opinions and try to bring out what they think." Wrote another girl, "In our daily lives we show that work is not something reserved for the poor . . . they know that we don't mind sweeping the floor, carrying water, gathering firewood, or doing our own dishes. This may dispel some of their own ideas about Americans, but our main point is that they should realize their own dignity." A volunteer wrote at the end of his service, "I hope that Filipinos have seen that whether a person works for me or is my superior, whether he wears a *sutana* or a *barong Tagalog,* I treat him with respect and equality." From the province of Negros Occidental, where volunteers brooded about the great gaps in wealth between the rich sugar *haciendemos* and the poor barrio farmers, another girl wrote, "Perhaps the concept of equality of opportunity— you are what you make yourself—is the most difficult part of Americans for Filipinos to understand."

And perhaps *utang na loob* was the most difficult part of Filipinos for Americans to understand. *Utang na loob* was at the heart of the Filipino way of life. Such ideas as personal independence and equality of opportunity had little or no meaning to the vast majority of barrio farmers whose earliest infant and child care and whose cultural ideals promoted harmony in interpersonal relationships based on a hierarchical network of obligations. Independence implies an explicit (or frank) assertion of self, even in conflict with others. Nothing could be more antithetical to the most basic feelings of Filipinos. Equality of opportunity is premised on conditions of opportunity which are unknown in the experience of most Filipinos.

Most lowland Filipinos (the vast majority of the population) are raised from childhood with two preeminent beliefs: anyone who hurts a member of his own group (it could be a large extended family or even an entire barrio) has committed a grave offense; anyone who does not defend his group against the insults or aggressions of outsiders has also committed an unpardonable offense. Aggressive behavior within the group (even words or looks) is highly discouraged.

One study of child-rearing in a Luzon barrio not far from Manila which had been more exposed to western and especially American influences than most barrios showed how extensively mothers discouraged independent, competitive, and aggressive behavior while encouraging dependence, obedience, and sociability.[2] As opposed to stressing independence training as in the American middle classes, Filipino mothers told stories of heroes who went home to seek the help of their mothers when in trouble. They also trained their children to be obedient. They made it clear that children were bound to follow their parents and that the oldest siblings were expected to lead their younger sisters and brothers. In the household there was none of the ambiguity of authority that obtains in American middle-class families. Most parents demanded obedience when they gave orders. Not a single mother offered a bribe or dropped a hint to obtain a desired action

2 *Maria Fe E. Abasolo-Domingo, "Child-Rearing Practices in Barrio Cruz Na Legas." Unpublished thesis, University of the Philippines.*

from the children. Outside of the immediate family, there was another hierarchy of authority based not on achievement but on the level of blood relationship. As opposed to encouraging individual achievement, the people of the barrio did not openly favor competition. Attempts to get ahead of one's peers were viewed negatively, and the vast majority of mothers placed little or no emphasis on their children becoming leaders. Mothers were happy to have their children perform the tasks assigned to them in the family and at school, but most of them were satisfied by any effort and were tolerant of inferior performances which they did not even bother to correct. A large majority of Filipino mothers did not permit aggression of any kind by their children. Most mothers acutely feared that their children would get into fights with playmates, and they told their children to withdraw when provoked. When asked to describe undesirable playmates for their children, not a single mother described children who were stupid, lazy, deceitful, unhealthy, or unclean. Every negative description with the exception of one (playmates who talked of "cheap" things) had to do with aggressive or quarrelsome behavior. Nothing was more important to these mothers than the ability of their children to have harmony in all their personal relationships.

In the Philippines, sociability is not just a matter of being friendly. It is sometimes a question of economic and physical necessity. Because resources are scarce, members of the group are taught to help and give protection to each other when danger comes. Children are trained to help younger siblings and to share food and toys with them. When they grow to manhood, they borrow from one another during times of need and return what they borrow when prosperity comes. But sociability brings its own rewards. As soon as the child is old enough, often about six months old, his mother may take him with her to the public market or when she goes to wash near the public faucet. If there are older siblings, they come too, and the children interact with others in the barrio in an atmosphere of high sociability. At almost any time of the day, but particularly after work is finished, they will sit on benches in the plaza, or, if the barrio has one, in the *lamyaan* (a shed with a platform; in literal translation, a place for rest) where they may also have a community radio. There they will talk, sharing gossip and information. If one has been to town or even for a walk, the others will ask for a detailed description of his experience. The feeling of being intimately linked to the fate of the group, which begins in childhood, rarely leaves barrio Filipinos.

PAKIKISAMA

The Filipino emphasis on harmony within the group leads to a pervasive personalization of life. Personalization has two fundamental aspects, one of which most volunteers never accepted. It is the emphasis on who one is and who one knows in the accomplishing of tasks and in the distribution of favors and privileges. The other is a high degree of sensitivity to feelings of anger and aggression in others and a strong inhibition of feelings within oneself that will hurt others in order to avoid quarrels and conflicts. Getting along with other people becomes the primary goal of life, not material possessions, education, or any assertion or fulfillment of self. It was this aspect of personalization which eventually had a profound effect on many Peace Corps volunteers.[3] To Filipinos, getting along with others often meant going beyond obligations fixed by role and status. It meant the enjoyment of people and relationships for its own sake. It is what the Filipinos mean by the word *pakikisama*, an expression of the desire to make another happy (come along with me, let's go along together, let's be happy together) and by the phrase *basta ikaw*, which means, "For you I'll do anything." After many months not all but many volunteers could appreciate the Filipino say-

[3] *See chapters 5 and 6.*

ing, *"Bisan saging basta labing,"* which means, "Even if we have only bananas, as long as there is loving."

As far as most volunteers could see, loving in the Philippines was related to survival and restricted to one's group. One did not usually love strangers unless they were powerful and prestigious like *americanos,* who could give protection and largesse. Other outsiders—the Muslims from the south, even people from another barrio or family—often were viewed suspiciously. To Western eyes, it seemed incredible that Filipinos, who gave each other so much within their restricted group, would be indifferent or hostile to children or persons in trouble who did not belong to their group. Volunteers frequently observed that "parents do not care for children unless they are their own"; and were often shocked at what seemed to them to be the cruelty of Filipinos toward handicapped or unfortunate persons outside their own family. After describing an incident when children and adults laughed and threw rocks at an emotionally disturbed woman who was visiting his house, one unusually stable and positive volunteer queried, "How can I adjust to something like this?"

It was basically a question every volunteer would have to answer for himself. As Peace Corps Director, I did not ask them to adjust to cruelty or injustice but to try to understand it and to deal with it as they saw fit within the vague limits of their responsibility to the Peace Corps as a whole. But I did not have to live with what volunteers felt to be the extremely harmful effects of *utang na loob* in the barrios. We were all attempting to live out the ideals of our culture, but they were living deeply in another culture, not to study it as anthropologists do, but to come to terms with it in order to fulfill Peace Corps objectives and whatever private goals they had set for themselves. Each of us would have his personal crisis with one or more aspects of *utang na loob,* and each of us would have to decide how to handle it.

In my earliest visits to the field, I tried to teach a little in each of the first six grades in order to understand better the problems of volunteers in the classroom. In one mixed-grade class in the Bicol, the male teacher let me lead a discussion on social studies and current events based on a newspaper distributed by the Department of Education. About forty youngsters were crowded into a one-room screenless nipa hut. They seemed bright-eyed, eager, and playful as they answered questions with an assurance that astounded me. I was pleased, and they were happy. Afterward, the Peace Corps volunteer who had watched from a corner of the room told me that the teacher had passed notes and whispered answers to the students. They had not wanted to disappoint me, the Director of Peace Corps. They wanted to show me proper hospitality by doing the very things that I wanted most, getting right answers. By desiring our encounter to be smooth, harmonious, and happy, they were expressing *pakikisama*. The teacher wanted the meeting to go well for my sake, but also because he did not want to have either himself or his class shamed by a bad performance. It was not important whether the answers were really known. It certainly was not important as to how the answers were known. What mattered was that the prestigious guest was pleased and the "humble" hosts were not shamed.

Such experiences confused and hurt volunteers imbued with the cult of individualism. What was smoothness (hospitality or deference) to Filipinos was often plain dishonesty to them. The rhetoric of school officials and teachers in towns and cities particularly conformed to American ideals, and behavior in relationship to Americans often seemed Americanized. Wrote one volunteer, "Several of the superintendents and supervisors have disillusioned and embittered me because they have fooled me into believing that they were devoted to the same ideals . . . improved education, a more democratic way of doing things, etc. Actually they were using both their position and me to further their most important ambitions: quest for political power, wealth, or both." Another volunteer, a married woman, wrote from her tiny island that simple observation gave her radically different impressions from the talk of her teachers about "educational principles, morality of teachers, methods of teaching." The talk, she wrote, "is moralistic rhetoric which has no relationship to reality."

Many volunteers believed that either Filipinos were frequently dishonest or they confused appearances with reality. But Filipino praise of American ideals and values was often an expression of *pakikisama*. It was saying the things Americans wanted to hear. As a perceptive volunteer wrote, "In the practice of smooth interpersonal relationships, the Filipino does not consider it a falsehood to tell you what he knows you want to hear, as long as the friendship is kept."

To understand *pakikisama* in personal relationships was one thing; it was quite another to acquiesce in it when one's crucial values were at stake. The majority of volunteers did not encounter what most of them would have viewed as flagrant dishonesty but even when some did, they somehow realized that behind the Western rhetoric, the action itself, bound up in a substratum of Malayan values, reinforced by Spanish and American colonial rule, was for Filipinos, irrelevant to the issue of dishonesty as Americans know it, and was often an expression of *pakikisama*. The teacher who prompted his children to cheat in answer to my questions was, from his point of view, being hospitable, not dishonest. Builders and contractors who falsified delivery and completion dates were anxious not to upset volunteers or staff rather than to deceive them. Neighbors who made volunteers twist at evening programs or drink *tuba* against their desires wanted to show how much they could enjoy the *americanos*, not by making fun of them (although this sometimes happened), but by having them enjoy themselves Filipino-style.[4]

[4] *A clinical psychologist, Jaime Bulatao, S.J., Director of the Central Guidance Clinic at the Ateneo de Manila in the Philippines, has described the process of being Filipino to oneself and American to Americans as the "split-level personality" in an unpublished paper entitled,*

HOSPITALITY

The young Americans were often seen as celebrities and in most barrios and towns—there were exceptions—they were feted with unparalleled hospitality. Neighbors brought food, bananas, and sometimes chickens which they could not afford for themselves, in order to give hospitality. The volunteers were invited to weddings and baptisms, and soon they were asked to be godfathers and godmothers, even when they were Protestants. "It still amazes me," wrote one girl, "with what friendliness and hospitality the Filipinos treat us. . . . There is no limit to the sacrifices these people have made for us and the little things they have done to make us feel at home." Sooner or later many volunteers were deeply and favorably touched by Filipino hospitality as an expression of *pakikisama*. One boy wrote, "It is a tremendous feeling to have a place where the people make you feel so welcome and wanted." But most volunteers, especially in their early weeks, wished for less hospitality. While they acknowledged that good relationships with Filipinos were important, they wanted to be respected and appreciated for the help they had come to bring. A girl from a poor barrio in Samar wrote that she first

---

"*Westernization and the Split-Level Personality in the Filipino.*" Filipinos try to give Americans what they want in words but remain deeply wedded to a fundamentally Malayan culture which is at odds with American values at crucial points. Filipino pakikisama, even when expressed in what seem to be hypocritical, dishonest ways to Americans, is a perfectly appropriate manifestation of Filipino values. Filipinos have learned to give Spanish and American audiences what they want, but when the curtain goes down, they can peel off their Spanish or American roles. It is not that these roles are not a part of them. They are genuine expressions of their Filipino selves in relationship to prestigious, powerful outsiders. In short, Filipinos appear to be true to themselves while (from a Western point of view) false to others, making Shakespeare's Polonius seem culture-bound.

For excellent discussions (on pakikisama) see Frank J. Lynch, S.J., "*Lowland Philippine Values: Social Acceptance,*" and (on utang na loob) Mary R. Hollinsteiner, "*Reciprocity in the Lowland Philippines,*" in Four Readings on Philippine Values, compiled by Frank J. Lynch, S.J., Institute of Philippine Culture, Ateneo de Manila University Press, Quezon City, 1962, pp. 100–120 and 121–148.

believed she was getting somewhere when, "after a six-week library class, a mother of one of the children said that her boy came home every night wanting to read more instead of just commenting on how beautiful the *americana* is." She had not traveled to the Philippines to be told she was beautiful. Some volunteers even began to think of Filipino hospitality as an expression of selfishness "to make," as a girl on Panay put it, "them feel gratified that they are pleasing us," or as their method of enhancing the social prestige of the host. At its worst, the price of hospitality was being made to listen to obscene jokes (if one understood the dialect) or being mercilessly teased (if sufficient *tuba* or rum had been imbibed).

Despite the overwhelming desire of most Filipinos to make volunteers happy, they sometimes did the very things that made them unhappy. A young Baptist volunteer from Texas wrote, "That I don't drink, smoke, or dance and try to lead a Puritan-Christian life is really something beyond belief here. I am often made fun of. They are sure I am not happy and are continually trying to reform me by having me enjoy myself." He went on to say that because he resisted, their pride was hurt and that they considered him aloof and conceited. Most volunteers, ever anxious not to hurt the feelings of their hosts, accepted Filipino hospitality even when upset by it. "The faltering party drags on," wrote an extremely popular (with Filipinos) volunteer, "because no one wants to hurt the host's pride by leaving early." Parties, eating, and drinking were more important in the lives of most volunteers than they had ever been in the United States with its supermarkets and fancy restaurants. To many, the school system seemed to be a series of fiestas, programs, *meriendas*, and athletic meets, occasionally interrupted by classes and national examinations. Teachers were constantly asked to sell and buy chances to support fiesta queens, church repairs, and athletic contests.

CURIOSITY AND GOSSIP

Incessant curiosity was another expression of *pakikisama* to the extent that it represented the desire of Filipinos to be aware of the needs and feelings of the Americans in order to get along with them. To make sure the volunteers were happy, Filipinos self-consciously inquired: Was everyone treating him well? Did he like the place? Was he afraid of danger? Was the food adequate? and so on. When a Filipino asked a volunteer for the tenth time, "Do you eat rice?" it was his way of asking, "Are you pleased with us; are you happy here?" It was extremely difficult for Filipinos to believe that the answer was *really* affirmative even when the volunteer said yes (many times it wasn't); and they needed reassurance. It seemed incredible that these young Americans, far from their loved ones and away from the wealth of their countrymen, truly liked "the place" and their meager diet of fish and rice.

Curiosity was also a manifestation of Filipino amusement at the passing show of Americans, usually so fair of skin and tall. Children would grin broadly and call out, "Hey, Joe," or "*Americano.*" They would giggle and nudge each other and their parents would smile and exchange whispers as the tall, fair *americano* strode down the street on the way to school. The Americans were better than a motion picture, partly because they looked like the Americans in the movies, but perhaps even more because they sometimes behaved so differently. Volunteers continually complained of being stereotyped according to the images of Americans presented on the silver screen or—in some sections—by American troops in World War II. Filipinos seemed amazed that all Americans were not rich; that American girls were not all sexually promiscuous; that not everyone gets divorced in the United States; and that Negroes were Americans too. Volunteers were pleased to burst these stereotypes. Many of the boys surprised their barrio hosts, as one of them wrote, by "not smoking, not chasing their women, by being interested in agriculture, and getting out of the bus when it stalled to help push." These things never ceased to amaze most Filipinos in the barrios and they could not stop asking questions about them.

In part, curiosity was simply the expression of fascination which barrio Filipinos had concerning the habits of strangers who, in some cases, were probably the main topic of conversation for months. A married volunteer wrote, "The people are curious about our personal habits. Our helper brings home from the market the current questions: Do Mr. and Mrs. L. quarrel or kiss or sleep together? Have they practiced birth control for six and a half years? Do they ever *utot?* (Cebuano for expelling wind). Married volunteers were asked frequently about having or not having children, because most Filipinos expect pregnancy as a matter of course following marriage. A volunteer couple from northern Luzon wrote, "One of our greatest annoyances is the constant question, 'Do you have any children?' Upon hearing us answer negatively, they ask, 'How long have you been married?' We reply, 'Almost two years.' And then the people really begin to chatter away in the dialect. If you understand them, you realize they are saying things like 'Are you weak? Don't you know how to conceive? Don't you sleep together? Why don't you have children?'" This couple found that the best answer for them was, "Science. *Ammuni, egga* science." (In Ilocano, "We know how to have children, but we use science.") The answer usually ended the conversation or, in a few cases, stimulated further questions about birth control.

Some questions were asked, neither to be hospitable, nor to amuse, nor out of fascination, but for information. Many Filipinos believed that the volunteers had a great deal of information of value to impart. They wanted to know about the United States because they were genuninely interested in that powerful, wealthy country. Wrote one volunteer, "I now have a ten-minute lecture on many subjects including marriage, divorce, courting, and standards of living. I really enjoy correcting badly misinformed people and . . . trying to live up to being an authority." But many volunteers, at least for the first year, were upset by incessant questions, especially when they came from better-educated teachers or lawyers. It was sometimes annoying to be asked by a local fisherman in the barrio if Americans ever ate rice or whether all Americans were rich; it was invariably unnerving to be asked the same question by a college graduate in the *población*. One volunteer from the Bicol wrote, "I get tired of continually repeating that I have learned to eat rice, that I have not yet found a wife among the many beautiful ladies, and that I really do not have a favorite movie star." When curiosity assaulted the volunteer's sense of privacy (even extending in some cases to reading the volunteer's mail), it was especially disturbing. That was particularly true of girls who, tall, fair, and independent (wanting to live alone in many cases), were subjected to strong Filipino curiosity. In a burst of frustration, one of them wrote that while curiosity was understandable up to a point, it was outrageous for people "to endlessly look in your windows, scale the wall to look into the bathroom, climb on top of the church or fence to see you." She felt that she had been "put into a showcase on display for two years."

Another aspect of Filipino life closely related to curiosity is gossip. Since it is extremely difficult for Filipinos to express hostility toward each other directly, they frequently vent their negative feelings to a third or fourth person. To talk about others to their faces would be intolerable; to talk behind their backs becomes a national preoccupation in a highly personalized society where the principal recreation is talking. To individualistic volunteers who valued frankness as a way of expressing individuality, gossip by Filipinos about Filipinos was annoying, but gossip by Filipinos about volunteers themselves was sometimes deeply frustrating (even though volunteers constantly gossiped about themselves). Volunteers who lived together usually were expected by their neighbors to do the same things and to travel together. When they behaved differently, comparisons were made. If one volunteer seemed to show more zest for Filipino food or to be more adept at the dialect, his housemate would be disparaged. Gossip about the alleged misbehavior of women volunteers was particularly irritating to the girls concerned, but it was so persistent and common that it was believed frequently by other volunteers hundreds of miles away and even by visiting officials from Washington.

DEFERENCE

There were three other qualities of Filipino life that affronted the individualism of volunteers. They were deference, possessiveness, and authoritarianism. Filipinos are accustomed from birth to the idea that interpersonal harmony depends on every man knowing his place in relationship to those above and below him. To most Filipinos, Americans are, by virtue of their wealth, power, and former position as colonial rulers, at the top of the ladder. Many Filipinos constantly deprecate themselves to Americans, showing deference and sometimes even obsequiousness ("I'm so ugly, Mum, and you're so pretty"). They put themselves in the position of lowly supplicants for favors and protection. There were exceptions, especially among the proud young students at the University of the Philippines in Manila and at other universities, the Muslim population in Mindanao and the Sulu Archipelago and, to some extent, the tiny Protestant population, but most Filipinos in the lowland Christian barrios viewed themselves as inherently and inevitably inferior to Americans.

American products, from songs to cigarettes, and American tastes, habits, and opinions commonly were imitated, as were the volunteers. To their faces, everything about the *americanos* was admired: fair skin, hair, and even the shape of their noses. "The little girls in my barrio school even imitate my hair style and shade themselves from the sun with big black umbrellas so their skin will be like mine," wrote one volunteer. To be imitated was upsetting to many volunteers (although it was flattering at first to some) since they wanted nothing more than for Filipinos to develop a sense of their own independence and a feeling of equality with others.

To be treated as a special hero by children could be deeply gratifying, but to be constantly deferred to by status-minded Filipinos, including teachers and school officials, usually was unnerving to volunteers with a passion for the ideal that every man should feel as good as every other man regardless of the condition or place of his birth. It was disturbing to an insecure and inexperienced Peace Corps volunteer to have older teachers defer to him at the slightest hint or suggestion (even though volunteers wanted to be taken seriously) because of his feeling that deference came not as a matter of conviction but only because of the status of the volunteer as an American.

Deference displayed (sometimes ostentatiously) by middle-class Filipinos was particularly disquieting since they often were more status-conscious than farmers in the barrios, for whom they would show disdain when extending sympathy to volunteers for having made "such a sacrifice by living with the barrio folk." Sometimes volunteers were puzzled as to whether Filipinos were simply telling them things which they thought would please them or actually believed the things they were saying, as when Filipinos told volunteers that they favored reincorporation of the Philippines into the United States either as a state or a colony.

On occasion fantastic requests were made, indicating a genuine belief that the Americans were truly supermen, as when, in the words of one volunteer, "a brown-skinned Madonna asked a blond Theseus to kiss her bulging belly to ensure a lighter-skinned, more beautiful, and socially attractive offspring." There were even instances when male volunteers felt they were being tempted or prodded by older people in the barrio to have sexual intercourse with their daughters in the hope of producing a half-American child.

"Leave our barrio a souvenir, sir," they would say with a broad, flashing grin. "It would make us proud!" Such instances were rare.[5] More common was the consant stream of self-deprecatory remarks or observations lauding the superior technology and wisdom (sometimes they seemed to be equated) of Americans.

Deference to volunteers was frequently accompanied by feelings of expectation. Because they were Americans, they were deferred to; but because they were Americans, they were expected to pay for the hospitality and deference shown by Filipinos—if not in cash and material things—by allowing themselves to be displayed and even possessed by their barrio neighbors. It sometimes took a while for Filipinos to realize that the volunteers were not "rich *Americanos*." They had more money than most people in the barrio (their salary was 212 pesos, or approximately 60 dollars, a month, the equivalent of other elementary school teachers), but in many cases they had just enough money to make ends meet each month. In some instances, when Peace Corps checks were mailed late by the U.S. Treasury Office in Manila or were delayed in the mail, volunteers were down to their last few centavos. The cost of living varied in different sections of the country and even between towns or barrios within the same region, and with careful management some volunteers saved money each month, which they often gave to help set up scholarship funds or for some other charitable purpose; but most volunteers, unlike the Americans of the movies, simply were not in a position to be big spenders, a fact of life which sometimes led to misunderstanding with Filipinos who expected *utang na loob* in pesos and centavos in return for hospitality and deference. When a volunteer requested the building of a dugout boat by a local carpenter, the Filipino smiled and said he would be happy to do it as a favor. The volunteer, unwilling to have the man work for nothing, ascertained the going price for

[5] *They also may have been magnified by volunteers.*

the work performed and offered to pay that amount for it, but the carpenter was insulted because the "rich *ameri-cano*" would pay no more than an ordinary Filipino.

POSSESSIVENESS

Most Filipinos quickly learned that *utang na loob* could not be extracted in money, but they expected volunteers to pay for *utang na loob* from Filipinos by letting themselves be used, even possessed, as status symbols. Volunteers claimed they were used as pawns of social climbers and complained about barrio neighbors who sometimes asked for things such as household items or clothes but more often merely wanted to display their volunteer. In its most common and mild form, possessiveness usually meant showing off a volunteer at fiestas or local dances. At its worst, it meant being used for financial or political purposes. "One evening last week I was invited by a head teacher to go with him to visit a few houses in the community," wrote a volunteer from one of the eastern Visayan Islands. "It turned out to be a fund-raising campaign, and I learned later that the purpose of my being there was to shame people into making larger donations."

Another volunteer, boarding with the relatives of important officials in the provincial school office, was told by his hostess that she did not wish him to pay her for room and board. (The volunteer insisted on paying as a matter of Peace Corps policy.) Later the hostess, in contravention of a public school rule which makes it illegal for close relatives of school officials to sell insurance to teachers, and who had earlier complained about corruption among government officials, asked "her volunteer" to accompany her when she sold insurance to teachers in the district.

A volunteer in the Bicol was caught in a fight between the local priest and mayor, both of whom tried to use him for partisan advantage. The issue arose when the mayor decided to change the date of the town fiesta in order to help promote business at the cockpit. The priest maintained that it was wrong to change two hundred years of tradition. The fiesta should be held on the town's patron saint's day, and at no other time. When the mayor held his fiesta in defiance of the priest, the cleric denounced him from the pulpit. In retaliation, the mayor began his own Sunday night gatherings, which included a short talk by him, songs, and a dance. For the second of these programs, the volunteer was invited as a guest speaker. Before he arrived at the meeting, the mayor blasted the priest (who was in the audience) for obstructing progress. The following Sunday morning the priest, in his weekly attack of the mayor, accused the volunteer of siding with the mayor. The volunteer, wanting to extricate himself from the conflict and to protect the Peace Corps, visited the bishop to inform him that he did not care when the fiesta was held and that he was not on anyone's side. To prove it, he attended the regular fiesta on the patron saint's day, made a stop at one of the local convents, and shared a drink of scotch with the priest, to whom he repeated his desire not to be used by either side in the conflict. It is difficult not to oversimplify the challenge in human relations which confronted the volunteer. From the point of view of mayor and priest, each of whom had performed favors for the volunteer, he was obligated to them. He believed it was important not to acknowledge his obligation to either one but also not to hurt their feelings or shame them in any way by giving too sharp a rebuff to their entreaties.

SHAME

The technique of shaming in order to enforce acceptable behavior is as appropriate to a society which values group harmony and cohesion as the inculcation of guilt is for American society which values personal independence.[6] As

[6] *Shaming is perhaps more common in the United States than most volunteers realized, especially in subcultures of poverty and immigrant subcultures, but it does not have the significance it has in the Philippines.*

Americans, Peace Corps volunteers experienced a considerable amount of guilt for feelings that were not supposed to be felt, doing things they were not supposed to do, or failing to do others which, by their own standards and that of their culture, they were supposed to perform. Guilt is a function of one's own internalized standards of right and wrong, and while it can be triggered by the opinions or behavior of others, it can exist without them, and often arises from the desperate, lonely feeling that, despite the praise of others, one has failed to live up to one's opportunity for choice, achievement, or moral behavior. While guilt is the primary means of forcing adherence to cultural values in America, shaming is the principal sanction in traditional societies which emphasize group harmony or cohesion. When a Filipino child transgresses, he becomes the target of scorn and derision and is made to feel embarrassed and shamed.

The subtle complexities of shame in the Philippines (*ulao* in Cebuano and *huya* or *hiya* in Tagalog) are extremely difficult to understand (and I am certain there is much I do not understand); the feelings that go along with being ashamed are a mixture of fear, anxiety, shyness, and embarrassment. There are, I am convinced, kinds and degrees of shame. In its mild form it is an accompaniment to the deference that is shown foreigners and persons of high status. It is an expression of embarrassment and shyness appropriate to one's status and situation: a family who sends a visiting volunteer to use their cemented washhouse rather than their bamboo toilet; a family eating supper on the floor of the kitchen with their hands, quickly drawing the curtain in order not to be seen by a volunteer; Filipinos in the barrio saying they are ashamed to visit the city; or a Filipino protesting that he is ashamed to go swimming with an American volunteer.

In other expressions of shame, the components of fear and anxiety seem more intense. It is not so much a matter of expressing one's identity, but of protecting it, as when the teacher helped his students in answering my questions in order not to be ashamed as well as to please me; or when, as happened in one case, a district administrator asked teachers to cheat on the national and division examinations so that the district would have good standing in the eyes of his superior; or when the people of one small, poor barrio were ashamed to face their two female volunteers after there had been a mass stabbing in their town (the mayor asked them not to tell anyone else what had happened).

In other, even more extreme cases, the fear of losing face becomes a more total fear of an unrecoverable loss. In such instances Filipinos attempt to avoid being shamed as though their lives depended on it. Such shaming can result from insult to family, *compadres,* or oneself, or even, in unusual cases, from being "stared-down" by another Filipino.

A few volunteers found the shyness aspect of shame attractive (one said he was happy to work with children who were more sensitive to feelings than frank, precocious American children), but a large majority of them saw shame as stifling the individuality of Filipinos, particularly the children in school. Children who did not learn quickly frequently expressed their shame by sinking in their seat as far beneath the desk as possible or, if they were larger children who could not fit under the desk, by hiding their heads behind an arm placed on top of the desk. Teachers sometimes expressed their sympathetic sense of shame and relieved the anxiety of such children by ignoring them, whereupon they were eliminated from the ongoing life of the class. If called to stand and recite, other classmates often came to their rescue by supplying whispered answers from every corner of the room, which the teacher usually heard but politely ignored in order to maintain the illusion that the child produced the answer himself. Thus the child was spared the shame of failure and even his classmates and teacher were spared unpleasantness. Sometimes a child struggling for an answer was shamed with nervous giggles or laughter instead of being helped with a whispered suggestion. Occasionally teachers would shame an entire class, who would then let their heads sink slowly to their breasts, and cup them in their hands.

AUTHORITARIANISM

What made shaming particularly upsetting to many volunteers was that it was a principal method by which persons of high status enforced their authority. Superintendents shamed principals, principals shamed teachers, and teachers shamed children. Against his strong belief in individualism, the volunteer was confronted with a society and a school system which put a premium on individuals knowing their place as subordinates in relationship to their superiors, and on suffocating individual innovation and initiative lest it be "wrong."

Authoritarianism meant—from the point of view of most volunteers—that superiors could exploit subordinates mercilessly. They frequently "asked" for contributions for favorite causes and charities; occasionally they made interest-bearing loans, against the rules of the Bureau of Public Schools; in rare and extreme cases, salaries were withheld. Often superiors imposed educational decisions against the judgments of teachers.

A volunteer on a much larger island was called into the office of her superior one day and told that she had to pass four seniors who were failing. "I went home stunned and prepared exams for all of them," she wrote, "but three of them failed the new exams." Her superior said the pressure came from higher up and that she had feared that someday something like this would happen. There ensued a long talk about ethics and education. Her superior, miserable at the confrontation after months of happy, harmonious friendship with the volunteer, ordered the grades changed against the volunteer's protest so the children could be promoted. She avoided the volunteer for days, turning away unhappily whenever she came into view. Later, after graduation, she apologized and promised she would never do such a thing again. To prove her sincerity, the superior talked to her Filipino teachers and told them she would never again ask them to change grades.[7]

Another volunteer reported, "Every teacher in my school deeply believes in this (program), but if our supervisor mentions a different idea, all of them will jump for it." There were many exceptions, teachers who did innovate and even dared to criticize, but inhibitions on such behavior were considerable. Teachers were easily transferred by superiors, and they feared being stranded in barrios dozens of kilometers from the nearest road or far from their home province. Mostly, they accepted—not always without discomfort— the authority and sometimes the bullying of their superiors without protest. In some instances there seemed to be little choice, as when a principal called in a sixth-grade teacher and ordered her to make the principal's daughter valedictorian, despite the fact that she rated about eighth in the class. If the teacher defied her superior, she might not have a position the following year. The daughter's grades were raised and those of the "true" valedictorian were lowered. The principal, apparently not caring that all the teachers knew what she had done, even gave a party in honor of her daughter. The volunteer attended, confused and upset, but unwilling to interfere. "If I had done so," she wrote, "it would have been messy for all concerned."

In an authoritarian culture education had an entirely different meaning from what it had to militantly equalitarian Peace Corps volunteers. To them, as they repeatedly wrote and said, education was concerned with developing the ability of an individual to think and reason effectively. In the Philippines, education meant collecting facts and degrees. "Here one must know the answer," wrote a volunteer. "One

[7] *The word "superior" is used purposely to disguise the kind of school we are talking about. It could be anything from a four-grade primary school to a college. In this case the friendship between the volunteer and her superior was renewed and deepened after the incident.*

must consult the authority on any given subject and if the individual is not in agreement, he must then alter his opinion to fit that of the authority."

The concept that authority is a source of knowledge discouraged the approach toward empirical learning in which volunteers believed. They were particularly dismayed by the heavy reliance on rote memorization. A woman volunteer wrote, "In science, the teachers taught the children to memorize rules about health habits which were meaningless because there were no toilets and in some cases teachers didn't have them." The problem was particularly serious in the teaching of science, which was characterized by the teacher's recitation of definitions and terms which the students committed to memory. Original answers would be considered wrong. Volunteers who tried to introduce an inductive approach to science (nearly all of them did) through experiments and demonstrations were fighting not just a system of authority in the schools, about which teachers and even principals (and sometimes children) occasionally complained, but an entire way of life from which most people drew security. The teaching methods of volunteers and their approach to learning sometimes challenged that security. "Because we allow the students to express themselves freely and to ask questions and criticize us in our homes," wrote a girl from the island of Catanduanes, "this is carried over to the classroom to the surprise and chagrin of some of the teachers."

ENJOY, ENJOY

Education is a primary instrument of socialization, and the schools in the Philippines and the United States express and reinforce the values of their own culture. Volunteers wanted Filipino children to think independently. Their coteachers, more often than not, wanted them to learn the obligations of *utang na loob* and the pleasures of *pakikisama*. That is why Filipinos repeatedly made it plain that for them the main job of Peace Corps volunteers was to enjoy themselves and enhance pleasure for those around them rather than disrupt the fundamental ways of the school system. Of course high education officials would always agree with my slogans about "creative children," "independent thinking," and "inductive science," but when I was honest with myself (and there were moments of self-deception), I realized that with the exception of a few subject matter specialists, they rarely raised these issues themselves. Time after time the deans of normal school and the top officials at the Department of Education would tell me that the Peace Corps was a wonderful program because volunteers seemed to be enjoying themselves. They participated in dances, fiestas, ate the native foods, and even intermarried. These were the primary concerns of even Manila-based officials. Nothing was more difficult for volunteers to understand or accept than that Filipinos wanted them for pleasure in relationships and not to achieve the tasks to which they had been assigned. Filipinos cared about the volunteers in their way as persons. So they stared at the *americanos*, asked questions endlessly, and surfeited them with hospitality. The supreme value of life was neither in being independent nor in productivity. It was in the enjoyment of relationships.

Behaving independently helps Americans to feel self-sufficient, frank, and competent. To Filipinos, the same behavior sometimes makes Americans seem to be unaware of their obligations, insensitive to feelings, unwilling to accept established practices, and downright aggressive. Compared to Americans, Filipinos undoubtedly see themselves as aware of their obligations and sensitive to the feelings of others. To volunteers, it often seemed that Filipinos wanted to be dependent on others and have others dependent on them; were ashamed in the presence of strangers and authority figures; were afraid of being alone or of leaving their families and communities; showed extreme deference to superiors and expected the same from subordinates; veiled true feelings and opinions in order not to hurt others or be hurt by them; attempted to manipulate other Filipinos or volunteers covertly without incurring *utang na loob;* and gossiped depre-catingly behind the backs of other Filipinos and volunteers.

Imbued with the ideals of their own culture, the volun-teers came to a land that had for more than fifty years given verbal endorsement to those very same ideals while retain-ing a way of life at variance with them. Of all the challenges set before them, this was the most difficult one that Peace Corps volunteers had to face.

IV
This thing
called culture

: Volunteers had expected to confront the physical hardships of Peace Corps service with rugged, self-confident de-
termination, and most of them succeeded. Most of them
were pleased with the natural beauty of the Filipino countryside, and were gratified at the personal cleanliness of
many Filipinos. But many were truly shocked by living in a
culture of poverty for the first time, even though they were
unwilling to acknowledge their feelings of revulsion until
after they had learned to live with them. But the fact of
poverty and its consequences—bad sanitation, poor health,
and physical ugliness—were ever-present. There was for
some a sense of shock in the appearance of "starving dogs,
sore-ridden children, spitting women, constant lice-picking."
As one boy wrote, "My being felt repulsion and I wanted to

draw away." A girl who eventually enjoyed and appreciated the Philippines and Filipinos with sensitivity admitted, "When I arrived here nothing appealed to my sense of taste —not sights, nor sounds, smells, food. . . . I felt completely cut off from anything I have ever known, and came as close as possible to having a nervous breakdown without actually cracking up." She concluded, "When faced with rotten teeth, foul breath, smells, sores, filth, rags, I couldn't take it. I was astonished to find that my reactions were so diametrically opposed to my ideals. . . . I simply and truthfully hated it all, wanted to go home, and the only thing stopping me was pride." Another volunteer wrote of his early months: "I spend much of my time looking for places to urinate, being angry with the presence of mosquitos, and some flies. I am constantly annoyed by spitters and careless coughers. I request napkins in vain and eat and drink the most disagreeable concoctions sometimes until I can explode." Poverty and differences in food and habits combined to cause severe discomfort only for a minority of volunteers.

CULTURE FATIGUE

Within several months most volunteers became accustomed to the physical aspects of life in the barrios (and some were never disturbed). That the beach was used for a toilet was accepted as a matter of course. That Filipinos frequently spit was less upsetting to them than the spitting of Americans had been to Charles Dickens on his visit to the United States a little more than one hundred years before. The constant diet of fish and rice was tiring, and some volunteers craved for peanut butter and crackers or other food favorites when they were unavailable, but the meanness and the sameness of food was not a major cause of the culture fatigue which overtook most volunteers by their fourth or fifth month of service. The major factor was not sickness, poverty, the absence of running water or electricity, or mosquitos. It was loneliness in the face of pervasive cultural differences.

The strain of being alone for long periods of time, the absence of personal friends who shared the same interests, having to respond over and over again to the same questions, suffocating one's individual preferences and opinions in order to please Filipinos, the tension of being stared at or being put in a high position and given privileges, and the petty inefficiencies and delays of daily living pressed relentlessly on the equilibrium of Peace Corps volunteers. It was impossible to reconcile the rhetoric of Filipinos about sanitation and hard work with their actions. A teacher who preached from a hygiene textbook spit out the window while the lesson was being conducted. Some girls who fancied themselves with elaborate dresses for the barrio fiesta defecated on the beach. A barrio lieutenant who spoke loudly of the need for better nutrition winked when powdered CARE milk was used for lining an athletic field. A principal who prated about the value of education locked up brand-new textbooks behind a glass-enclosed case to show them off. A young boy who claimed to love the Peace Corps *americano* continued to call him Joe for days on end, even though the volunteer begged him not to. A farmer who encouraged the volunteer to practice medicine to help improve the health of the children in his barrio went to a local *herbolario* to obtain urine for his pinkeye and a poultice of leaves and dirt for his cuts. A woman next door who went to Catholic Mass every day lived in dread fear that sea monsters shaped like short, black, slimy men would pull her fisherman husband to the bottom. Even when these apparent anomalies could be explained by *bahala na* or *utang na loob* or the culture of poverty or by the sociology of rural life, they were depressing for many volunteers, especially during the first year, and their cumulative effect produced not a sense of shock but of emotional fatigue.

One of the most upsetting aspects of life in the barrio was

the laughter of Filipinos at someone who was hurt. To volunteers, Filipinos often seemed more concerned to place blame for an accident than to show sympathy and give assistance to the victim. Wrote one boy, "Countless times I have witnessed injuries during athletic meets greeted by gross inaction and a chorus of laughter. When a girl I had worked with sprained her ankle in the broad jump and began to cry from the pain, . . . not one spectator lifted a finger to help her but they merely tittered and pointed at her. Bloody noses seem to be a cause for special hilarity as are broken fingers." Another wrote, "A kid in my school could have bled to death (when a section of a wall creased his forehead) while the teachers were busy placing the blame on the carpenter that built that particular section three years ago." At least as disturbing as laughter at accidents was the widespread Filipino acceptance of death. One girl wrote, "While sitting through a novena feast for a friend who has just passed away and listening to all the laughter and gaiety, I am completely baffled for I cannot understand how people can laugh at death." Puzzling at the indifference to the drowning of a seven-year-old child, a volunteer wrote that he wondered why men were made so different "until I got a headache from wondering."

From day to day, it was neither death nor accidents which were most culturally fatiguing to volunteers. It was *bahala na* in the schools which made volunteers feel they were standing still or moving backward in their work. The feeling, as described by one boy, was like "running an efficient sailboat, and then pulling down the sails in a good wind to scrub the deck and paint the hull for the captain's approval; then setting sail and furling again to review and memorize the manual for the captain's quiz. You know where you want to go; yet it is maddening to be dropping anchor so often." How could they help the people progress, volunteers wondered, when "fear," "lethargy," "self-doubt," "passivity," and "a lack of self-confidence," as they put it, dominated the lives of Filipinos.

Most volunteers, including those in the first group who had received the least effective training and field support, and who were guinea pigs in the development of the program, conscientiously persisted in trying to contribute to its overall objectives despite culture fatigue. Many of them were emotionally exhausted after four for five months. A female volunteer wrote, "It was rather like pouring water into a sieve." Another extremely dedicated and determined girl wrote, "I feel very small and weak in the light of this thing called culture and its strength." In retrospect, the vast majority of volunteers showed amazing persistence and courage in coping with fatigue. At one point, perhaps as many as one half of the first group of 128 volunteers would have resigned if they could have done so with honor. Those were tense, frightening weeks for me when it was necessary to persuade volunteers of the importance of sticking it through, even when they were exhausted and depressed.

INDEPENDENT FEMALES

While most aspects of *bahala na* and *utang na loob* affected nearly all the volunteers, there were special characteristics of Filipino culture which made unusual difficulties for young women. There are few things more strikingly peculiar about American culture than the assertion of independence and equality by unmarried females. Foreign visitors to the United States always have been astounded by the degree of freedom of movement and choice given to single girls. Having chosen to live and work in a small village many thousands of miles from home, female volunteers constituted an unusually independent group of young women. So strong was the desire for freedom of movement and privacy, even from other volunteers, that by February, 1963, more than one out of every six girls (a total of fifty-nine) had split off from their households and were living alone—usually with a Filipino helper, sometimes with a Filipino family, and occasionally by themselves.

The drive for personal self-sufficiency presented serious problems in a society which tended to interpret the independent behavior of young women as a sign of sexual promiscuity. Filipinos, at least ostensibly, tend to think of two kinds of girls: the protected and unprotected, or the nice and not so nice. Although there is some variation from region to region and barrio to barrio, respectable Filipina girls usually are not permitted to leave their homes on their own. If they travel any distance at all, they have to be accompanied by a companion. After sundown, girls are not allowed out of their houses except when there is a town dance party, or some special religious affair. At such occasions they are protected by companions who are constantly at their side. Dating, that extraordinary and originally American institution (now catching on in some parts of the world), is rare in small rural barrios. American young men and women, insisting on their right of free mate choice, threw off the institution of chaperonage before the eighteenth century. Eventually the exploratory, experimental, unchaperoned relationship known as the date took its place.

In the rural Philippines, girls are courted by serenaders (usually after they have received permission), who sing outside the girls' homes at night. Filipinos repeatedly made it clear to volunteers that "good" girls were never seen alone with a male, because when a man and a woman were left together alone the only possible result was sexual intercourse. (They were little aware of the extraordinary range of male-female interactions from bundling to petting which had been developed over the decades in the United States.) To protect the *americanas,* Filipinos often told them to close their windows and not to go out at night. In a few cases, boys were not permitted to serenade the girls without getting permission from the mayor or barrio lieutenant. In a *población,* teachers and school officials might become more upset when a female volunteer went walking alone than in the barrio, where they were usually accompanied by children, who could provide companionship without curtailing freedom.

Most girls learned that they would be permitted freedoms not allowed Filipinas. Many of them did go for walks alone, usually to the market or to a neighbor's house, sometimes even at night, and some went swimming without older companions or Peace Corps boys to accompany them. In several cases, Filipino serenaders were invited into the homes of Peace Corps girls for small, informal parties. These things, never done by Filipinas who wished to protect their reputations, were often accepted by Filipinos. "Americans are like that," they would say. But many Filipinos never lost their sense of concern and distress at displays of *americana* independence. They worried about girls who entertained men without the presence of vigilant mothers, aunts, grandmothers, or older cousins. They were confused by the informality of clothes worn by Peace Corps girls. In one instance, two girls in a small town in Zamboanga del Sur wore Bermuda shorts to the plaza after having been reassured by a Filipino host that it was all right. The girls felt they were undressed by the hopeful, probing eyes of the young men and humiliated by the disapproving looks of all others. To guard the Peace Corps girls against such embarrassment, the Director of the Bureau of Public Schools advised provincial officials to watch them "protectively from a distance as wise parents watch grown-up daughters" in order to protect them from barrio gossip.

But protection was often impossible. The American girls repeatedly invited the predatory attention of Filipino men through carelessness, and sometimes perhaps even intentionally (however subconscious). They were vulnerable, not only because they resisted protection, but because they were big, fair, and generally thought to be attractive. They had been preceded by American movies, which, through Filipino eyes, depict American girls as loose and easy to get (and sometimes sex-crazed). They lived in a culture which embraces a strong, pervasive double standard giving considerable sexual license to young men who are free at a level below the ostensible norms (at least of the Catholic Church, if not of barrio life at a deeper level) to violate systematically those norms.

In the early weeks, volunteers often gave the wrong cues to Filipino men because of their strong desire to show goodwill toward everyone in the barrio or town, as well as to maintain a certain degree of independence. They did not usually realize the extent to which men are not considered responsible for their extramarital sexual actions in Filipino villages. The girls had lived with a double standard in the United States but nothing like they encountered in the Philippines, where married men often openly acknowledged their mistresses and bragged of their sexual prowess with many women. Many volunteers in extremely small, remote barrios found that there was considerable sexual freedom for both sexes, perhaps related in some deep and persistent way to the Malayan culture of previous centuries in defiance of the norms imposed by Catholicism, but most volunteers encountered a powerful and pervasive double standard comparable to that in the Catholic countries of Latin America; and within that framework, American girls frequently were thought to be available.

Annoyances ranged from stares and insulting remarks to touching, pinching, jostling, and (rarely) more frightening overtures. No Peace Corps volunteer was ever attacked in the Philippines, but they were frequently annoyed. The stares and remarks were upsetting even when they were understood as part of the culture. One tall, redheaded girl wrote that she could understand why she was insulted by young, unemployed, *tuba*-drinking Filipinos when she strode through the barrio on the way to school, but she was still hurt and felt powerless to do anything about it. Another acknowledged that the Filipino male cannot help but become more familiar with an American woman than he ever would with a Filipina. They want to touch and pat *americanas*, believing them to look something like Elizabeth Taylor or Marilyn Monroe and expecting, or at least hoping, that they will behave as their movie characterizations. Another wrote, "I could explain their behavior in terms of the culture but this doesn't make it easier to know and enjoy them." Said another girl, "When I'm alone and men yell, I still feel a little squeamish and sometimes even unclean." At a barrio dance Filipino men (often married) sometimes insisted upon close bodily contact or cheek-to-cheek dancing, which they would never do with a Filipina who was under the watchful eyes of her parents. When they thought about it, volunteers realized that some of the same kind of advances would be made in rural communities in the United States if they moved in as strangers not knowing how to define the situation in order to protect themselves. Just as *americanas* have a reputation in the Philippines, big-city girls have a reputation in rural communities in the United States. The problem was how to defy that reputation and yet retain one's independence and compensate for the deep loneliness and isolation which they felt.

For boys, it was much easier to give up normal dating and to conform to the Filipino way. It was easier to give up dating probably because many of them found, as men usually do in the United States, outlets in their work, athletics, and male camaraderie. There were many things they could do which female volunteers could not: play basketball, run up and down the beach, and even drink *tuba* with the boys. It was easier to conform to the Filipino way of courtship partly because it was the only way accepted by respectable, marriageable young women. I know of twenty-three male volunteers from the first nine groups who married Filipinas after having followed (in most cases) the cumbersome, family-involved procedures of wooing and winning dictated by Filipino culture.

A majority of girls were often upset by their relationships, or lack of them, to Filipino men. A typical barrio had few Filipino men over eighteen or under forty who were single and eligible from the point of view of the girls. But the desire for close relationships with men was present. One girl wrote about the extreme loneliness of barrio life. "As the loneliness deepened, the need to have someone hold your hand, put his arm around you, maybe kiss you, was very strong." She wrote of "an emotional vacuum that craves filling," and "the deepening of a friendship that I knew was wrong . . . giving and receiving on almost all levels of intimacy." Such friendships, even when they did not involve sexual intimacy between American girls and Filipinos, often were assumed by Filipinos to be sexual. Another girl became good friends with a woman and her twenty-nine-year-old bachelor son who, although there was no romantic involvement between them, was the best friend she had in the Philippines. Because she was open about her affection for him, the volunteer was the target of what seemed to her to be vicious gossip in the town.

Gossip, a major social activity in the barrio, often focused on sex. Some men had more than one wife; men who called themselves single frequently were married; marriages often took place after pregnancy; and so on. Without much else to do for diversion or entertainment, gossip about sex was unavoidable. Women volunteers agreed that the gossip heard about them was often centered on Filipinas, too. Many had heard "malicious gossip" concerning Filipino teachers. Yet when it applied to them (and almost always it was exaggerated or even absolutely false), it hurt deeply. Many volunteers whose behavior was impeccable had been the victims of upsetting rumors which, when they were lucky, made them tearful for a short time, and when unlucky, plagued them for months.

There were variations in the behavior of Filipino men toward female volunteers. In Muslim communities girls were bothered much less than in Christian barrios because of the strong Muslim taboos against looking at or touching women. Also, some girls found that as they became more involved in their communities, insulting words and actions practically ceased altogether. There was general agreement that a female volunteer in a larger *población* had more trouble because it was more difficult to define her relationship to strangers and to receive protection than in a smaller barrio.

There also developed a growing competence in dealing with the problem. Some girls invented fiancés in the United States. Most became circumspect in drinking, smoking, and dress. While not allowing themselves to be possessed by their protector—an official, a school principal, or an old lady next door—volunteers learned how to depend on them. Some found that by moving in with a family they could define their situation as protected. Nearly all of them avoided traveling alone unless necessary. Some passed the word through friends, sponsors, or companions that they would not dance with drunks or married men. It was often enough to explain, "It is not my custom." Volunteers learned how to find out which of the men who called themselves "single" actually were married and which were "negotiable" or really single. They found out that if they refused an invitation from one man to dance, it was wise to turn down all others for the same dance. It was difficult not to accept an invitation to dance with the mayor or doctor, even if they were married, but one could learn to say that more than one or two dances was too tiring or pretend an inability to follow. Some girls became more confident in reprimanding dancing partners who used "fresh" language, although they tried not to be overheard in order not to shame the Filipino. They became more forceful at holding the dancer at arm's length, realizing that they did not have to "get along in the community" or "be friendly to everyone" at the expense of their personal integrity.

Despite the persistent frustration over gossip, stares, insults, and touching, not a single female volunteer left the Peace Corps because of it, although it may have been a contributing factor in a few separations. Much more serious was the problem of loneliness and the profound need for male companionship. Many factors led several girls to fall head over heels in love with Filipino men: the extreme loneliness of their situation; the extraordinary flattery and attention heaped on them by Filipino men; the relative lack of experience of the girls in dating and coping with the same kind of attention back home; the feeling on the part of some of the older girls (the average age was twenty-four) that opportunities for romance and marriage would soon be dwindling; the extreme social and intellectual isolation of volunteers, which made a male Filipino with ambition or intellectual pretensions seem unusually different and attractive; and the search for adventure which brought many volunteers into the Peace Corps to begin with.

From the point of view of the staff, such romantic attachments, even when they led to marriage, as they did in thirteen cases during my period as Director, often meant trouble. There were exceptions, but female volunteers in love with Filipinos hurt the Peace Corps in various ways. The mildest and least important problem was that they became targets for gossip. In many cases they became less conscientious in their work. In some cases their behavior was, from the point of view of Filipino and Peace Corps standards, irresponsible enough to lead to their separation from the Peace Corps. Of the twenty-three girls separated from the Peace Corps during my tenure as Director, five of them resigned because of frustration and fatigue; four quit to get married; two already were married; two suffered severe psychological difficulties; and ten were separated for misbehavior connected with romance and sex. Of those ten, four married Filipinos and continued to live in the Philippines, but the conduct of their courtship was sufficiently problemful as to limit their continued value to the Peace Corps. By contrast, not one of the four male volunteers separated for misbehavior had a history of romantic involvement in the Philippines, and not one of the twenty-three boys who eventually married Filipinos was obliged to leave the Peace Corps because of misconduct or allegations of misbehavior during courtship. Culture fatigue clearly had special meaning for the girls.

COLOR IN THE BARRIOS

There were special problems for Negroes in the Philippines. They were stared at even more than other volunteers. They realized soon that a vast majority of Filipinos placed a high value on light-colored skin. "I felt like a specimen in a test tube," wrote one boy. "Everywhere I went, people pointed or made comments about the pigmentation of my skin or the texture of my hair." Some Filipinos would ask Negro volunteers if they were truly Americans. They found it inconceivable that white and Negro volunteers lived together (the Army in the Philippines was largely segregated during World War II and racial tensions were often high). Occasionally, well-meaning individuals would approach a Negro volunteer to ask him to state his grievances against the white man.

Nearly all volunteers, but Negroes especially, were upset by the Filipino preference for light-colored children. Darker offspring were frequently discriminated against in the distribution of clothes or privileges. Some white volunteers found it hard to convince Filipinos that they were not prejudiced against color and that they did not believe Negroes to be inferior to whites. "After refusals of sun umbrellas, hats, and a shady seat, and after taking 'baths in the sea' at noon and displaying my ever-improving tan," one volunteer wrote that her neighbors were beginning to realize that she really did admire darker skin. But most of the thirty-three Negro volunteers in the first nine groups were insulted in ways that were difficult for their white friends to understand. They were met with the salutation "nigger," in some cases for months after children and neighbors had learned their names. A teacher friend of one volunteer suggested that he post his name on the house because the children really believed that his name was Nigger, a theory confirmed a month later by a little boy who answered in response to a question that the volunteer's name was just that.[1]

It is impossible to sort out the sources of Filipino color prejudice. In part, discrimination against persons of darker color stems from the Spanish and American occupations, but it may even predate the Spanish regime with its association of light color and high status. Whatever the source, most Negro volunteers were disturbed. Several resented the invidious comparisons made between them and white volunteers behind their backs by Filipino teachers or neighbors. They hated the comparisons made between themselves and other Negroes who were of lighter or darker skin, always in favor of the lighter colored volunteer regardless of individual merit. A Negro boy overheard an argument by two Filipina teachers, one of whom complained because the Peace Corps had sent a Negro volunteer to their school; her colleague answered back it was better to have a Negro who teaches well than a white teacher who is ineffective.

For the most part, Negro volunteers were able to break the pattern of gossip and discrimination as they became close personal friends with teachers, children, and neighbors, but not without having been hurt in the meantime. They tried to cope in different ways. One girl ignored every taunt for three months and was miserable most of the time. One boy forced the issue whenever he had an appropriate opportunity. At teachers' meetings he argued that it was unjust to discriminate against darker-skinned Filipinos. He exposed himself to the sun and said he was proud he was a Negro. Southern Negroes seemed to cope with hurtful remarks better than those from the North. Perhaps light-skinned and usually better-educated northern Negroes, struggling with their own identity at home, felt the hurt more. On the whole, most Negroes did amazingly well, and

[1] *I doubt that most Filipinos who use the term do so maliciously or even with hostility. To them, I think, it is purely descriptive. A boy with a limp might be called Gimpy in the barrio. A boy with effeminate characteristics would be labeled accordingly but not pejoratively.*

only two, both of whom were light-skinned and came from predominantly white communities in the United States, had to be separated from the Peace Corps. Nearly all the others, particularly the Southerners, showed extraordinary resiliency and strength in dealing with the frustrations of intercultural conflict.

THE CHURCH IN THE PHILIPPINES

Catholic volunteers, men or women, Negro or white, also had special problems peculiar to their own background. The Peace Corps, with its secular missionary emphasis, was expected to draw heavily from Protestants in the middle classes. Yet many Catholics from lower middle-class backgrounds joined the Peace Corps. Although no statistics were taken, my impression is that approximately 40 percent of the six hundred volunteers who served with me were Catholic, and a surprising number were ex-seminarians.

They came to the Philippines at a time of extraordinary ferment within the church in America. Self-criticism on every issue from birth control to parochial schools was widely heard. John F. Kennedy, the first Catholic to be elected President of the United States, emphasized the importance of separation of church and state. John Courtney Murray, America's leading Catholic theologian, was working out a new concept of the rights of conscience as opposed to the traditional view that error has no rights. The Catholicism of the Philippines was to a considerable extent a result of the legacy of pre-sixteenth-century Spanish Catholicism imposed by sword and mission on top of a Malayan folk religion which had proved absorptive and adaptive. It was an authoritarian, superstitious, and almost medieval Catholicism from the point of view of many Americans who experienced it in the barrios.

Church and state blended easily in a variety of ways despite formal restrictions to the contrary. Dominican priests came into the public schools to drill children in their catechism. One volunteer told of a visit on a Saturday morning to a first-grade room where she met with ninety other teachers in the district, all standing in a cramped position to receive the local priest and about a dozen matrons of the Women's Catholic League. Introduced by the District Supervisor, the priest explained that he needed money for a beautiful new church. He hoped they would contribute generously even though most of the teachers in the district lived and worked away from the *población* and could not attend Mass in the new church on Sundays without traveling a full day. His plea for voluntary contributions was met with silence. The District Supervisor exhorted the teachers to contribute to the project despite that section of the Code of Professional Ethics for Public School Teachers and Officials of the Bureau of Public Schools which states that no school official should directly or indirectly solicit money for any political or religious purpose. Under pressure, according to the volunteer, the teachers finally agreed to contribute one peso a month for as long as it would take to pay for construction of the church.

Many Protestant volunteers were upset by such tactics, but others found the mystery and symbolism and passion of Filipino Catholicism to have elements of attraction. It was mainly the Catholic volunteers who were disturbed by corruption in the Church. To hear a priest use vile language, to know that a priest had several children in the barrios, to hear a rumor that a priest had broken the seal of confession, to see Catholics who believed more strongly in ghosts and spirits than in the teachings of the Church—these things were upsetting to many. One Catholic girl wrote, "When you see so many people not practicing what they vehemently defend as their sacred belief, it becomes a source of great frustration and even intolerance." Another wrote, "I have seen the onslaught of the old emotional religion with its claims on the poor. I must come out for a reform of the Church in any country where it suppresses them." Still another said, "Here in this Catholic country, it seems to me to be all hypocrisy, bowing and scraping and crossing oneself, without any meaning behind this outward show." Several volunteers were forced to reexamine lifelong beliefs. "I came to the Philippines a Catholic, but everything here seems to work against Catholicism as we Americans understand it. . . . As far as religion goes, I now think I should term myself 'an American Catholic.'" There were exceptions even among Catholics, and there were many who were largely indifferent to the discrepancies and peculiarities in the Catholicism which they found in the Philippines, but at least as many were upset.

The focal point of annoyance was usually the priests, many of whom admitted openly that they had been forced into the priesthood at an early age by zealous parents, and who seemed indifferent to the vital needs of the barrio people with whom volunteers were most concerned. Some volunteers saw the priest in the Philippines as an authoritarian, status-ridden functionary who believed in the laws of his superiors but not in the spirit of Jesus.

FIGHTING FATIGUE

The overriding contributor to emotional fatigue in the Philippines was the conflict which volunteers felt between their desire to show friendship and goodwill toward Filipinos and their deeply negative feelings concerning the effects of *bahala na* and *utang na loob*. The very quality which Filipinos often praised in Americans—frankness—was the characteristic which hurt them most, and volunteers knew it. To be quiet in the face of what volunteers perceived as dishonesty or even authoritarianism and sloth was, in the view of several, a compromise with one's integrity. In extreme cases the conflict led to emotional and physical collapse. One girl, who saw smooth interpersonal relationships as leading to "corruption and soul-slavery," battled for her survival as an individual. After more than a year of personal crises faced with courage and ingenuity, she was plagued by bad diarrhea and sleeplessness. "I know that the diarrhea was not caused by something I had eaten or drunk," she wrote. "For the first time in my life I was all nerves; my stomach was in knots. I paced the floor for three or four hours." Although she went to bed at 10 P.M., she could not get to sleep for five or six hours. Sheer courage often kept her from being defeated by such punishment. She kept trying because, "I feel that to a greater degree than ever before in my life, I am deeply involved in something that is truly significant . . . so don't worry about me. . . . We asked for it and we are continuing to ask for it. This is a rich experience for us, and the fact that it sometimes is dark and painful and highly frustrating doesn't detract from any of the richness, so long as we survive, and I think we will."

GUILT AND RESENTMENT

The physical and emotional malaise of volunteers resulted only in part from culture shock (the early reactions to poverty and a strange environment) and fatigue (the longer range reactions to cultural conflict). It also derived from the volunteers' sense of guilt stemming from a feeling that they had let themselves, their country, and the Philippines down. Most volunteers had set high standards for themselves, reinforced by Peace Corps advertising and the pressures of training. Freed from the restraints of academic and bureaucratic life in the United States, they expected to test their mettle and hoped to accomplish much. They also fervently wanted to show their love for mankind in practical, day-to-day ways. When frustration led to helplessness, volunteers felt guilty. One girl who started to sleep late in the mornings (this was true for several during periods of acute culture fatigue), and spent only an hour or so in school for almost an entire month, wrote, "My conscience bothered me constantly. I had guilt feelings because I knew that I was sleeping late every day."

Advertised as self-sufficient supermen, many volunteers

themselves at first believed the propaganda. But when faced with unanticipated obstacles, most volunteers were often quite needful. While never recanting their ideological commitment to self-sufficiency, a large number of them asked for more support. They complained of not being adequately trained. They often asked for more equipment and supplies. They wondered why overseas staff members could not visit them, and they were bitter about the slightest administrative holdup. They doubted if Sargent Shriver or the Washington office really cared about them and their frustrating work in the barrios. But many of them resented help when it was given because it betrayed just how difficult it was to fight against emotional and psychological isolation in a new and difficult job in a strange and disorienting culture. They did not want to need help; and they were uncomfortable about their dilemma.

They also felt guilty because the combined pressures of their own achievement drive and the expectations and hopes of the American people for the Peace Corps did not seem to be matched by accomplishment. Volunteers were expected to perform like Homer Atkins in *The Ugly American*. In appealing to potential recruits, the Peace Corps emphasized the opportunity for significant work overseas; recruits were encouraged to believe that they would serve in the front line of America's missionary effort for peace and freedom. That was especially true for the earliest volunteers who, long before they reached their villages, often were billed as a new kind of American hero who would perform valiant deeds for less fortunate peoples.

As the volunteers settled into their villages, newspaper and magazine articles at home and abroad continued to emphasize their alleged brilliant successes. Most volunteers felt it was impossible to be as sacrificial or as successful as the publicity indicated. Already deeply anxious about their capacity to do an effective job (for many it was the first job, for all a new one), they often felt guilty knowing their achievements fell far short of the effervescent publicity.

"Washington does not help the volunteer by the propaganda it insists on churning out; and when the first realization hits that you are not all you're cracked up to be, or that you can barely begin to make all the contributions that you once thought you could, there is a tremendous let-down," wrote one volunteer. But it wasn't all Washington's fault. The American people and their newspapers and magazines wanted to believe the best of the Peace Corps. They purposely ignored mistakes and failures because it meant so much to them to have the Peace Corps succeed. One girl wrote that she was depressed "to see one's own picture in a national magazine and to read that one's youth, energy, and American ingenuity were uplifting a particular group of students or teachers or rice farmers." A male volunteer said, "I'm sick and tired of reading stateside papers my parents send me which contain nothing but positive comments about the work of the Peace Corps." A boy who failed to develop a sense of effectiveness in his job until his second summer, when he worked at an educational summer camp which he helped to plan, acknowledged that without the camp which he thought was successful because "it was of a concrete nature, something that a volunteer could devote time and effort to just as he would in the States," would have left the Peace Corps feeling that "I had betrayed the people of the United States who accept so willingly the Peace Corps volunteer as indispensable to the country of his hosts."

The applause given to volunteers came from Filipinos, too, and that was another stimulus to guilt. The outpouring of praise for Peace Corps volunteers in Filipino newspapers and magazines and in the speeches of politicians was based in large measure on a sincere surprise at the extraordinary capacities of volunteers to adapt to Filipino life and in delight at their transparent goodwill. It was based also on simple Filipino hospitality. These young men and women were Kennedy's representatives. Thousands of Filipinos believed they had been sent personally by President Kennedy as a

gesture of friendship to the Filipino people, and they reciprocated with lavish praise appropriate for representatives of
the highly admired President of the United States. But Filipino praise at the local and provincial levels sometimes was
based on the hope that voulnteers would bring tangible
benefits; and municipal and barrio councils not infrequently
commended volunteers for their contributions even before
they had made them. At town fiestas volunteers were celebrated as great heroes even when they had done virtually
nothing up to that time. Filipinos, out of a sense of hospitality, sometimes praised volunteers for projects which had
proved impractical and perhaps were unwanted. One boy
wrote that he appreciated the thankfulness of Filipinos,
"though it makes me also feel guilty that I have not yet done
anything to deserve their thanks."

Guilt was mixed with resentment and discouragement. A
boy wrote, "We are embittered by facile self-congratulation
and the persisting inaccuracies in depicting our experiences
on which the public praise rests. We know it is b.s. and we
feel used." The pressure on the first groups was especially
strong. "It seemed we were being lionized before we had
done anything and I resented references to our courage and
sacrifice," a girl commented. Small triumphs were blown up
out of all proportion by visitors from Peace Corps in Washington and newspapermen. A Peace Corps official, who saw a
girl make mats out of a fiber that had not previously been
used for anything in particular, reported to Washington that
a new weaving industry was on the way in the Philippines.
That kind of exaggeration, often used by agencies to justify
their existence, was especially hard on the volunteers who
needed more than anything else to learn how to wait for
results. One boy astutely saw that the Peace Corps was more
than just another agency to the American people. It was a
basic expression of national values and character. "There
seems to be a tendency," he wrote, "to regard the volunteers
as a kind of front line in the holy war of human development."

MOTHER PEACE CORPS

The vast majority of volunteers eventually dealt construc-
tively with their feelings of frustration, guilt, and bitterness,
but not without a considerable struggle and a displacement
of these feelings with expressions of hostility toward the
Peace Corps in Washington, the staff in the Philippines,
other volunteers, and even Filipinos. The hostility toward
Washington was based in part on the volunteers' resentment
of Peace Corps public relations which one volunteer saw as
a playing up of the "mock heroics" and the "soft soap and
hard sell." But it cut more deeply than that. Many volunteers
felt that the Peace Corps in Washington cared more about
congressmen than Filipinos or the ideals of the Peace Corps.

It was false dichotomy based to a considerable degree on
the lack of political sophistication of Peace Corps volunteers.
To make Peace Corps ideals operational, it was necessary to
have the support of Congress, and Shriver's brilliant performance in winning the support of senators and representatives, while accomplished without sacrificing those ideals,
was appreciated only by a minority in the earliest groups.

The remoteness of Washington made the Peace Corps
there an easy target for verbal aggression. Visitors would fly
in and out of the Philippines in a few days. They made a
short trip to the field, spending ten or fifteen minutes at a
household, or in some cases staying overnight. Although
many of them understood perfectly that they could not appreciate the depth and complexities of the life of a Peace
Corps volunteer in the barrios, they usually were charged
with superficiality and sometimes even a lack of concern
(criticisms justly earned by some).

Both the Peace Corps in Washington and the staff in the
Philippines were resented also for establishing policies and
regulations for volunteers to follow at the same time that
they extolled the self-reliance and individualism of Peace
Corpsmen. To volunteer for Peace Corps service meant to
commit oneself for two years in pursuit of basic policies set

down by Congress, interpreted by the President and Sargent Shriver and administered by overseas staffs. It meant obedience to policies, rules, and job responsibilities and a persistent commitment to promote the good of the Peace Corps as a whole. Volunteers were not like other volunteers who usually do not depend upon an organization or institution for housing, food, medical care, equipment, and supplies, and who are not selected under rigorous procedures following a ten-week or three-month training program. (As many as 40 percent of the volunteers scheduled for service in the Philippines were "selected out" of some training groups.) A Peace Corps volunteer is a special kind of volunteer. He works for the federal government; he signs up for two years; his housing, medical care, and living expenses are taken care of; he has seventy-five dollars a month saved for him by the federal government. During all his waking hours he is subject to the discipline of Peace Corps rules and regulations and Peace Corps staffs which interpret them.

The main job of the staff overseas was to provide support, but that sometimes meant establishing policies and regulations too. From the volunteer's point of view, whatever helped him to achieve effectiveness was good administration. Whatever hindered him in achieving that objective was bad. Volunteers needed certain basic medical and logistic support and help in gaining an increased understanding of and control over their job responsibilities. While I believed that regulations should aim at giving support to the volunteer in overcoming difficulties and ameliorating pressures to free him to use his own resourcefulness, it was sometimes necessary to impose rules for the good of the Peace Corps as a whole: where they could travel and when; how they could spend their free time and summer vacations; how they could dress in some cases; how many hours they had to spend on the job. In the Philippines, certain hotels and restaurants were put off limits. Discipline was rare (and many volunteers urged that it be stronger for those who were rumored to be misbehaving or performing their job in a lackadaisical way), but it was bitterly resented when applied. When one member of my staff sharply criticized two girls for going to Manila without permission in order to raise money for their summer camp, one of them wrote to me to complain that other volunteers were roaming the island without opposition from the staff.

It was widely believed that the staff played favorites in picking Peace Corps volunteer leaders (who functioned in assistant staff capacities) and in extending privileges to some volunteers. The staff was accused also of being inefficient when the forwarding of mail was delayed or monthly checks were not disbursed on time (sometimes this was due to inefficiency but rarely). The staff in the Philippines was criticized, no matter how desperately it tried, for not visiting volunteers in their barrios and for not staying long enough when they did visit. Dozens of volunteers were stereotypically adolescent in their relationships with the staff. They wanted to be free; but they also wanted understanding, support, and praise. When praise came, it was sometimes resented as out of proportion and as lacking in appreciation of the deep frustrations felt by volunteers.

Because of the early hair-shirt Peace Corps philosophy, staffs were kept small. Before leaving for the Philippines, I battled in Washington to increase mine to five (including a medical doctor), a ridiculously small ratio for the three hundred volunteers planned for the first year. By the time I left the Philippines, I had an American staff of nine for six hundred Peace Corps volunteers, the lowest staff-to-volunteer ratio in the world. Because of problems in travel and communication, it was impossible to visit households often or to stay long. I visited the household of every Peace Corps volunteer from group one by traveling four days out of each week for a period of five weeks. It was a physically punishing experience which could never be repeated for subsequent groups who usually met with me in group meetings set up in the field by other members of the staff. One girl wrote after that early trip that she was gratified that the staff was trying "to get to know the volunteers as individuals. I think we all dread the day when we might become just a number." A girl from the same group wrote months later that she wished the staff could come and take a look at their special summer project. We feel, she said, "unwanted, unhonored, and unsung."

Nothing was more important to me than giving closer, personal support to volunteers who needed it. What seemed to me to be stupid, unfeeling cables from certain officials would wait for replies when the morale, integrity, and health of volunteers was at stake. Socializing with officials from the embassy and AID was given low priority. Speechmaking was curtailed. Visitors from Washington were treated with cordiality but volunteers came first. Key staff members were moved with their families to live in the field to be closer to volunteers, and during my second year in the Philippines I moved my family to a crucial field location near Zamboanga (nearly 40 percent of all Peace Corps volunteers in the Philippines were in Mindanao at that time), where I established a Peace Corps field training headquarters (while keeping health and logistic support in Manila), in order to free me from the social and representational responsibilities in Manila and give more time to volunteers in the field and to a program which was badly in need of attention. As a consequence, I was able to spend about 40 percent of my time in Mindanao, another 40 percent elsewhere in the field, and 20 percent in Manila, where social demands and the expectations of Americans in business and government no longer interfered so strongly in my desire to give more direct program support to volunteers.[2] These steps helped, but for many volunteers, fighting against emotional

---

[2] *The move was not considered wise by all Peace Corps officials in Washington. Some thought it was a serious mistake not to spend more time in the capital city. Sargent Shriver backed the move after a visit to the Philippines. It is my opinion that communications with most of my staff, volunteers, and Filipino officials improved after the move.*

and psychological isolation in a new and difficult non-job in a strange culture, there could never be enough close, personal support and empathy from the staff.

FAMILY PEACE CORPS

Volunteers freely criticized other volunteers about as much as they did the staff. Anxious and insecure, needing realistic feedback on their performance (not trusting either the unstinting praise of Filipinos or Americans), many seemed willing (and even anxious) to make invidious comparisons between other volunteers. One mature and married male volunteer acknowledged, "I find myself inordinately interested in the lives and loves of volunteers I scarcely exchanged a word with in training." Rumors did much harm. So-and-so, it was alleged, had not been to school for a week. Did you hear that X had a nervous breakdown? Is it true that Y was seduced by the principal's son? It made little difference that X and Y lived hundreds of miles away. Rumors were greedily passed on and eagerly believed in periods of high frustration and low morale.

Fortunately, not too many volunteers turned their sense of frustration and guilt against themselves. It seemed to me better to have them complain about the staff than to punish themselves. Of the 630 volunteers who served in the Philippines during the first two years of Peace Corps operation, only four were returned home for serious psychological difficulties, and only one of these had been a complainer. That the main symptoms of culture fatigue were complaints which sometimes were based on rumor or fantasy did not relieve the staff of the obligation to deal with complaints and criticisms by trying to understand what lay behind them, as well as by trying to remove the specific irritant or problem which caused stress for the volunteer. But no matter what the staff did or did not do, we all learned that the goals of the Peace Corps were inherently difficult and stressful to perform. Demands were placed on volunteers which they had never experienced before and which few who had not experienced them could imagine. The deprivations they felt were primarily psychological, not physical, and it was a measure of the quiet, persistent courage of the vast majority of them that they achieved second, third, and fourth bursts of renewal after periods of deep fatigue and depression, and, in most cases, learned to cope with themselves, the Peace Corps, and that thing called culture.

V
With this understanding

: Most volunteers learned that the problem of coping with
the non-job amounted to learning how to live with Filipinos.
They discovered that while there was often an apparent
(and sometimes real) conflict between *pakikisama* and getting on with the job, that the effective transmission of skills,
and of the values to which they related, depended on their
acceptance of Filipinos as persons. In retrospect, that seems
obvious; but at the time, it often seemed as though *pakikisama* was a cultural conspiracy to prevent the volunteer
from helping Filipinos improve their education, health, and
productivity.

136

THE PROCESS OF COPING

Most volunteers, including those in the first group who probably received the least effective training and field support, conscientiously persisted in trying to fulfill the overall objectives of the Peace Corps program. The process of trying for most of them appears to have involved seven stages of reaction to and interaction with Filipinos and the non-job. These stages tended to merge into one another and did not always come in the same sequence; nor were they of the same duration. But the seven stages of coping usually appeared as follows:

1. The volunteer was curious and waited for signals as to what he should do.
2. He became impatient with the failure of Filipinos to give clear clues, and developed a strong desire to accomplish something.
3. He started projects in school and community, sometimes with apparent success, often with failure, and began to realize how deep are the problems inherent in fundamental change.
4. He discovered the Filipinos might simulate change to please him but that nothing had really changed.
5. He reacted by working harder and by trying to push Filipinos to accomplish things his way.
6. He felt depleted and defeated in the realization that pushing did not result in real change and that he remained a stranger in his barrio.
7. He began to accept and enjoy individual Filipinos for what they were in an almost unconscious recognition that any change in skills and abilities depended on changes in values, and that such shifts could not usually be effected by action or words except in the context of mutually accepting relationships.

Progression through these stages was often halting, and some volunteers, who mistook simulated change by Filipinos for real change, never passed stage three. There were steps backward as well as leaps forward, and for some, the fifth and sixth stages were skipped entirely.

THE EARLY TRIALS

The early waiting stage found volunteers saying, "I must try to understand the culture. I must watch for the right cues. I must remember I am a guest here." In the second and third stages, volunteers gave up waiting. Pressed for time, they began building science rooms, preparing English lesson plans, starting piggeries and poultry industries, building water-sealed toilets, inaugurating summer camps, libraries, and adult education classes. They had their share of failures. One girl kept some laying hens in a cage, but her neighbors did not think eggs were important to their diet and no one adopted the idea as she had hoped. The neighbors let their chickens run free and they were lost, stolen, or hit by a bus; they felt sorry because the volunteer's healthy chickens were cooped up.

Sometimes Filipinos responded to an innovation (or seemed to). They leaped at a new idea, praised it, and then acted out the Tagalog proverb on Filipino enthusiasm: "Like burning *kogon* grass, it flashes with a brilliant but brief flame, without sustained heat." One boy on the island of Bohol proposed adult education classes. The barrio seemed happily enthusiastic. He enrolled almost forty potential students and worked out a schedule suitable for all; but at the first class meeting he was dismayed to find the classroom empty. A group of girls in the province of Albay held adult education classes during the first summer vacation. Practically the entire town attended at the first meeting. At the second session the attendance dropped to one half. At the third meeting only about a third of the original group showed up, nearly all men. At the fourth session they had a class of ten; at the fifth, attendance was so slight they were forced to dissolve the class. One girl on Catanduanes decided that the solution to nutritional problems in her barrio was oysters. She had a meeting with barrio officials and everyone was enthusiastic. The local Bureau of Fisheries representative assured them that they would receive a truckload of free oysters. There was considerable excitement as they studied oyster-raising and discussed recipes. The oysters never came, although she later heard that some were sent to the governor's home town.

SIMULATED CHANGE

Volunteers began to realize that some changes were not really changes at all. "Sometimes I had the illusion that I was getting some of my ideas across," wrote one volunteer. She had thought that the teachers were really interested in her suggestions, but she later found out that they pretended interest either to receive favorable mention in an efficiency report or, more likely, just to please her. Another volunteer wrote, "The first month, I thought that my teachers really understood me . . . but soon I saw . . . they were too anxious to please me and often told me what they thought I wished to hear, rather than what they thought."

In order to please volunteers, Filipinos simulated change just as they had for the Spanish friars hundreds of years before and for American officials at the turn of the century. Filipinos had incorporated Spanish churches and American schoolhouses into an essentially Malayan culture, fitting Catholicism into a complicated polytheistic religion of ghosts and gods, and making the schools a place for public meetings, an important industry, and an instrument of political control.

With the realization that Filipinos did not quite understand what the volunteer meant by freedom, productivity, self-help, and creative relationships, came a better perception of what it was Filipinos did value and what they wanted from volunteers. Filipinos wanted volunteers to eat the local food, speak the dialect, dance the regional dances, give pleasure, and enjoy themselves. That was the way to show they really cared about the barrio.

THE AMERICAN STRUGGLE

Some volunteers who sensitively understood the fundamental nature of the value conflicts they faced were unwilling to accept Filipinos and their "wrong" values. They tried all the harder to fulfill the mission of America to bring technology and freedom to the Philippines. Still others leaped over the fifth and sixth stages to accept individual Filipinos for what they were. In the fifth stage, volunteers frantically tried to achieve something, anything, just to achieve. It was a time when gratification came from, as one of them put it, doing things "according to our own methods."

Then came stage six, a period of fatigue and defeat. "After a while," wrote one volunteer, "I reached the state of mind where I realized that it was impossible to fight back." The tedium of a non-job in a non-job culture was overwhelming. Volunteers complained of boiling their water, having to eat canned corned beef and rice, the buses, anything. But mostly they begged for work. The sense of defeat came even to some of the strongest and most sensitive volunteers. One of them, a girl in one of the Bicol provinces, had initiated a series of abortive projects. First there was a barrio cleanup campaign that she and two teachers started but which no one followed up. Then she began a project to build a plaza. That one lasted four months, with committees and subcommittees. The next project was a library. She wrote, "This time I was not to be caught. I knew the rules, I thought. Rule 1, only suggest, stay in the background. Rule 2, avoid leadership at all costs. . . . The project folded after five and a half months."

Defeat on the job was often accompanied by the enervating feeling that no matter how one tried, one always remained a stranger to the culture. One volunteer who felt at home in her barrio after five months left for an extended period to attend a language institute. She went home on a weekend during the institute to see her friends and try out her new vocabulary. "It was late in the afternoon when we reached C——; we turned down our road, the children swarmed, grabbed our suitcases, and the thrill of being home was strong. Then as we walked on and saw Mrs. P. with Junior at her breast and the flies buzzing over the back of F.'s carabao, I suddenly felt as though I were really a stranger in a foreign culture." Such setbacks could be as depressing as failures on the job, leading to an overwhelming feeling of tiredness.

ACCEPTING FILIPINOS

While there was no automatic formula for coping with the non-job or the non-job culture, it certainly had something to do with accepting Filipinos as persons. "Somewhere along the line," wrote one boy, "one finds oneself slowly accepting Filipinos on their own merits." One learned to be patient and to accept from the Philippines and Filipinos what they had to give and which was offered with generosity of spirit. Learning patience was a struggle. One volunteer on Cebu wrote, after reading about corruption in Manila and Cebu City politics, that he would "like to write some angry letters and make some angry speeches." He was furious about the educational system. "I think I could do a better job even with the little experience I've had." Then he caught himself. "Over and over again I realize you don't change an attitude that quickly or even with those methods. I have to keep telling myself that maybe I will change someone's attitude a little over a period of two years. . . . I'll really have to spend a lot of time with them and get to know them if I hope to."

A boy in the province of Camarines Norte told of a period of despair on the non-job which ended in a mood of acceptance. He came to the sixth-grade class where he planned to teach a new technique in the approach to oral

English, but the teacher was absent. Since the demonstrations were primarily for her rather than the students, he decided to wait until she returned. He passed the time correcting papers and planning future lessons, but she never arrived. He was next scheduled to teach remedial arithmetic to the fourth grade, but when he reached the regular room, he discovered that the students had been sent to another room to take an examination. His last assignment of the morning was to teach oral English to fifth-graders and arithmetic to a special group of third-graders, but he had to spend a portion of that period looking for a vacant room because the principal permitted a pair of clothing salesmen to use his arithmetic classroom as a display room.

"In spite of the minor inconveniences of the morning, my primary thought as I walked home for lunch was not about school, but how to get a cold Coke in order to beat the growing heat of the morning." He stopped in a half-dozen stores between the school and his house, but found that not one of them had bought ice in recent days. Feeling depressed, he went to the principal's office, where he learned that six of the fifteen teachers for the fifth and sixth grades were absent (four were attending a conference and two were ill). With feelings "bordering between disgust and indifference," he retreated to the small room in the central school which he had converted to an office. For about an hour he worked on his special extracurricular project, a five-year development map of the school site. Unable to make what he considered satisfactory progress, he threw everything into a drawer and stormed out of the door, marking the end of the school day.

"I was physically and mentally tired," he wrote. "I was hot and thirsty from my noon longing, and I was both disturbed and disgusted with the happenings at school. . . . I walked down the street with a chip on my shoulder and a scowl on my face, but before I knew it the whole environment acted as a medicinal: the smiles and greetings of the passing children unaware of my wrath, an invitation to play badminton on the town's new court, the reddening of the sky as the sun slowly sank into the sea, and the discovery of a store with ice," restored his equanimity and patience.

While the inefficiency inherent in *bahala na* could plunge a volunteer into despair, his spirits could be restored by an unexpected expression of *pakikisama*. A boy on Bohol went to visit a teacher about forty kilometers away, planning to come home the same day because he lived with four small children (temporarily adopted into his home) and did not want to leave them alone overnight. A bus driver friend had promised to pick him up on his last trip. He waited, letting several other buses pass, but his friend never came. Now forced to remain away for the night, he planned to return as early as possible the next morning because it was market day and he had to give the children money to buy food for the week. In the morning it took two hours before he felt he could excuse himself from his hosts and not hurt their feelings, but he had to leave. After hitching a ride on a truck which quickly broke down, he met friends who urged him to come to their house. They gossiped and ate until it was time to catch the last bus. It was dark when the bus dropped him seven kilometers from his house; but he was in luck. The driver of a truck promised to pick him up just as soon as he returned from a special errand. The volunteer went to the principal's house "to wait and wait and wait." Evidently his friend had forgotten him. The volunteer wrote, "The next person to say, 'You are making a big sacrifice,' was going to be told he was god-damned right. . . . And then I saw the truck racing back toward the *población* for me with a full load of passengers who didn't mind retracing four kilometers over a bumpy road at suppertime to reclaim one of their friends." The joy of seeing them and the fun on the way to the barrio reclaimed the day. *Pakikisama* prevailed.

PAKIKISAMA AND THE CHILDREN

The pleasure which Filipinos found in relationship came to mean a great deal to volunteers. In this, Filipino children helped considerably. From the beginning, most volunteers welcomed and enjoyed the children who came to their homes in the afternoons and evenings, played the guitar, read comic books, or talked aimlessly. Uncertain of their jobs and in relationships with adults, many volunteers turned to the children for satisfaction. Children, even when poor and hungry, represented hope. They lifted spirits with a giggle or smile, a present of fruit shyly offered, openmouthed amazement at the demonstration of electricity or of moon phases, twinkle-eyed joy at being able to say a whole sentence pattern in English and to use it in a real situation, and flustered excitement in searching the far corners of a world map. Nothing pleased the volunteers more than seeing youngsters discover or create something by themselves: the force of magnetism attracting a nail through a piece of cardboard; germs spoiling the fish inside the schoolroom while the fish drying in the sun remained unspoiled; drawing a picture out of one's imagination; sculpturing a wire carabao.

Children became the center of life for many volunteers who believed that it was too late to encourage initiative and creativity for teachers trapped in an authoritarian school system. The children were also just plain fun. They streamed through the homes of volunteers and, overcoming shyness, they borrowed classic comics, played *sunka* and checkers, and laughed and joked at their new friends from the United States. They gaped at the ingenuity of volunteers in designing science experiments or painting pictures out of native materials. They looked inside the *World Book Encyclopedia* in awe at the wondrous world which volunteers brought to the barrio. They "elevated your spirits," one volunteer wrote, "until you believed you were at least the equal of Captain Marvel."

It became apparent that one did not have to control the classroom as a teacher to have fun with Filipino children. Even an educational aide could enjoy and love them. "I love those children and they love me and that's the miracle which, had nothing else worked out, would have made those two years the best of my life," wrote a volunteer on returning to the United States. "Are all children as lovely and magical as Filipino children with their quick, shy smiles, and sloe-black eyes set in enchanted faces as old as time? What can it be about a mountain child in a tattered dress and mud-caked feet who, brushing the strands of jet hair out of her eyes, offers me her only food, a *camote*, wrapped in a banana leaf, which moves me so profoundly and makes such a difference in my life?" The answer, of course, was *pakikisama*, or a Filipino way of saying, "I like you and I want you to like me." The children—playing basketball or chess, making faces at each other, laughing at the halting efforts of *americanos* to speak the dialect—were balm for tense and disheartened Peace Corps volunteers. "Most of all," wrote a volunteer from Mindanao, "you depend upon the children for sustenance of spirit, the snotty-nosed, potbellied, dirty, half-starving, taunting, curious, wonderful, laughing kids." The children gave volunteers entrée to other relationships. "Because I love the children, I think the people opened their doors to me," wrote a girl from Negros Occidental.

It usually took longer for relationships with teachers, household helpers, neighbors, or other adults to provide joy. The process of becoming more accepting was slow, irregular, and uncertain. Volunteers did not say to themselves, "Now, I will become accepting." Volunteers who felt patience and openness growing within themselves would become frustrated and irritable again and then return to a more accepting mood.

ACCEPTANCE AND EFFECTIVENESS

Many volunteers began to see that without acceptance of Filipinos as persons, accomplishments on the job probably would not be lasting or significant. One girl wrote that "the *only* way progress can be made by Peace Corps volunteers . . . [is] by accepting Filipinos as individuals." Acceptance meant more than tolerance. Sometimes it led to caring deeply about the feelings of Filipinos. At least, it meant volunteers could participate in *pakikisama* on Filipino terms. Those volunteers who reported a sense of effectiveness in their work were, with few exceptions, the very Peace Corpsmen who learned to enjoy and care for Filipinos as persons.

One boy, for whom *pakikisama* and the job seemed compatible almost from the beginning, became one of the first volunteers to learn the dialect in his region, even using it to teach geography and arithmetic to adults. He enjoyed serenading at night with the gang from the *sari-sari* store, drank *tuba* with the older men who, as he put it, "had the pleasure of learning they could drink the American under the proverbial table." For him, work and pleasure seemed to merge. He wrote, "The older generation have had their stories of questionable conquests listened to . . . the teachers have had me as a captive guest for never-ending programs, and may have learned a little through my in-service training on English and science." Perhaps because he was willing to serve on every committee and come to every program, the municipal officials helped him in a cleanup campaign and even provided funds to finance his evening adult education classes.

Another boy, who had experienced a great deal of anxiety in training and felt extremely competitive and ineffective as long as he lived with other Americans, left his four-man household on the island of Panay and moved by himself to a smaller island one hundred kilometers north of the capital city. He wrote from his barrio, where he lived with a Filipino family, that "in many ways, living here has been something of a fight for survival . . . a foreigner cannot live and work here on his own exclusive terms." After eight months of service, while he was in the hospital with amoebic dysentery and bronchitis, feeling "pretty used up," he wrote, "it dawned on me that I would get nowhere beating my head against the wall . . . changes could possibly be made, but not in the way I was going about it."

Despite a busy teaching schedule, he organized an effective campaign to build outhouses, helped to begin a successful Red Cross blood drive, and conducted an excellent adult education course on health and nutrition. In retrospect, it seems that the key to his success was the extent to which he had become integrated in his community. "Even when school seemed to be going sour," he wrote, "I gained pleasure in living and being with these people." Nearly every evening he and his family would sit down together, drink *tuba*, talk and joke in a combination of English and Hiligaynon. "At times I was ill and both Y and Z would be awake all night in case I wanted something," he wrote. "Whenever I had been away for a day or two, my return was always greeted with smiles. . . . When I walked through our small barrio I could always count on people waving, smiling, and greeting me. Life on the island is hard; they know it and I learned it. For this reason, I felt that I was sharing something with them. . . . The people there knew I liked the place and liked them. . . . At times I have never felt more contented and relaxed, and of greatest importance to me are new bonds of friendship, respect, and love."

Perhaps the people of his barrio cooperated on his toilet-building project because they wanted to please him; perhaps they were ashamed to have him do the work. Whatever the reason, within two days after the volunteer built the first toilet, a neighbor started and completed his own toilet. Within five weeks the barrio people built a total of seventeen outhouses with only two shovels, one pick, and an iron bar. The new bamboo and nipa outhouses were used by the people in the barrio who now had more toilets than any of the nearby island barrios, three of which sent delegations to ask the volunteer's help in similar projects; and, most important of all, he did not have to do any of the work on the last sixteen outhouses.

Another volunteer spent a considerable amount of time attending barrio council meetings, P.T.A. meetings, graduations, teachers' meetings, bull sessions, stags, and social and political functions. "I feel that with a close enough attachment to people, through respect, friendship, and personal commitment, I can . . . do my very best," he wrote. He sang songs, danced, gave speeches, went to fiestas, laughed at unfunny jokes, made friends with old ladies, and talked with indolents; and people worked with him out of friendship because they did not want to see him unhappy or fail.

In his first few weeks in the barrio he suffered from "reformitis" and a desire "to change everyone and everything." Seeing the futility of that approach, he began "working on a small manageable scale," and with the cooperation of a shop teacher and a science teacher, who had been notorious for failing to contribute to school projects in the past, helped to build and equip the science room, revise the science curriculum in his school, and stimulate more effective science teaching in the district. With the help of the volunteer, the shop teacher became unusually productive and extremely proud of his accomplishments. (As for the volunteer, his friendship with the shop teacher became at least as important to him in the end as building the science room itself.) The barrio lieutenant contributed one hundred pesos to help finish the shop and new science room, and the P.T.A. reshingled the fifth- and sixth-grade building. The four English teachers with whom the volunteer worked enjoyed and used the new oral English teaching approach, and his visual aids and teaching devices were understood and employed. Later the volunteer saw his work in a new light, calling it "a new type of work, waiting sometimes instead of working, sometimes leading, sometimes at the sidelines, sometimes shoulder to shoulder."

Another volunteer, whose first reaction to frustration was to plunge himself into work, admitted at the end of his tour of duty that friendships had become more important to him than work. He was astonished at his ability to socialize. "There are picnics, jam sessions, parties, and just impromptu sessions of dancing or swimming. And on many evenings we just sit around and talk. . . . In all these relationships, the outstanding factor is friendship . . . and these persons are persons to me, not only Filipinos."

As he looked back on a successful working relationship with a coteacher, he found it hard to say where the work left off and the friendship began. "But I do remember one afternoon when she and I and another teacher sat talking for several hours after school was out. The conversation was personal. I think that our friendship has made her a more interested person—that her curiosity has been stimulated in a variety of things. She is now studying this summer in science, a field she was not especially interested in before . . . and is extremely interested in mathematics as well."

Another volunteer, whose achievement motivation was as strong as that of others who had a much more difficult time, began by enjoying the people of his barrio before he had any evidence that they would respond to his projects in and out of school. He made daily walks through his barrio, talking to people, practicing the dialect, and meeting the parents of school children. He stopped at the *sari-sari* store or dropped in on town officials and gave the impression of enjoying himself thoroughly. Within a year he had helped build a science room, revised the science program from grades one through six, introduced new mathematics techniques, helped to adopt the new guides for teaching English, and inaugurated a school newspaper. His students showed considerable improvement in English and science; the teachers with whom he worked began and ended school on time; and he helped to spark one of the more successful community libraries begun with Peace Corps help.

A boy who had started his service in the Peace Corps as an iconoclast became much more interested in people as he tried to work with them. He enjoyed fishing from a *banca*, plowing with a carabao, and building with bamboo, but, more importantly, relationships took on a new meaning. He wrote, "I used to think I could take people or leave them. They are more important now." His approach appears to

have led to considerable success in work. Through his initiative, stone walks were put in muddy places in the barrio,
two new toilets were built, a science room constructed, and
a compost pit begun. In addition to his regular school assignment, he conducted informal agricultural classes with
older students, introduced a few new vegetables in the barrio, and may have found a solution to the problem of tomato
blight and wilt. Farmers became so interested in his activities that they visited his house to ask for information and
bought seeds. Some even requested that he begin an adult
education course in horticultural techniques.

One female volunteer began life in the barrio by embrac-
ing *pakikisama*. "I was interested in their likes and dislikes,"
she wrote of the people in the barrio, "[and] what they
thought about the United States and how they were going to
accept me as a person, and not as a stranger who came to
make changes." She wrote that she wasn't in a hurry to find
their mistakes. "We worked slowly, and when we understood each other . . . working with the teachers proved to
be the most important thing to me in my stay in the Philippines. They were my best friends. After school hours, we
spent much time together, talking about the States and the
Philippines. I could go to them with any problem I had, and
they did not hesitate to come to me." She helped several of
her coteachers and her head teacher with new methods and
materials as she discovered that there was no conflict, at
least for her, between getting along and doing a job.

LIMITING GOALS

During stage seven, volunteers learned how to accept failure on the job as well as to accept Filipinos as persons. They
learned not to expect efficiency or even cooperation from
many Filipinos but to seek those qualities in a few persons
and to focus on a particular job in working with them. They
limited their expectations as well as their objectives. The girl
from Catanduanes who failed to introduce an oyster indus-

try because of political factors began to "question just how patient I was," and "found out that it is better to concentrate on doing one thing well than to do a half-baked job on several things."

As volunteers limited their expectations and focused their goals, they developed more confidence in their own ability to survive. After one year, a boy from Samar wrote, "I have become somewhat more of an optimist about what one person can do. It is vastly more important to work tenaciously on what you have and can reach than to bemoan inadequate preparation or vagaries of work." What were once considered small and insignificant accomplishments were seen as more important and felt as deeply gratifying. A girl felt a thrill of pleasure when "the most unresponsive child in school raised his hand to tell the answer to a science puzzle," and when a teacher from a rural school decided to continue teaching in the barrio instead of switching to the central school because the *Americana* had been willing to teach in the barrio. "These have been moments of gratification which more than make up for the endless days with few accomplishments," she wrote.

Another girl felt a sense of triumph because she persuaded her head teacher to let a nearly blind boy continue in school despite the fact that he would lower the class average on the national examinations. Another girl who taught an adult education class wrote, "I will never forget the time that Mrs. R. was so excited because she carried on a conversation with a doctor completely in English, and how Mrs. R.'s husband cried (he was a little drunk, but never mind) when she gave her graduation speech, and Mrs. S., who was my eldest student at sixty . . . what a thrill it was for her to give the first speech she had ever given." A boy from Bohol who had once dreamed of building dams, but gave up his dreams to become "a person to be listened to at meetings and a favorite at weddings and parties" felt a sense of achievement when in the summer, two months after school had let out, his children could still call after him, " 'Sister Susie sells seashells by the seashore,' without making a mistake or only a small one.'"

Whereas before the little disappointments became major frustrations, in stage seven the little accomplishments became major joys. After a year, a girl wrote to me that she was proud that she could hike twelve kilometers, eat rice and vegetables all week, carry her water in a bamboo tube, and bathe under a small waterfall. A boy who had earlier questioned the basic worth of teaching in the elementary schools wrote that he felt rewarded by "listening outside a classroom as a shy teacher secretly stumbled through a suggested science lesson; having a sixth-grader ask for a copy of *The Red Badge of Courage;* watching the amazed look on fifth-graders doing their first real science experiment; and seeing the hard-boiled mayor of our town wipe away the tears when we said good-bye."

ACCEPTING FILIPINOS AND BEING TRUE TO ONESELF

While *pakikisama* and the job were usually compatible, conflicts between them did occur, particularly when the demand on the volunteer to go along meant acquiescing in authoritarianism or what was seen as hypocrisy. Some volunteers felt caught in a constricting bind between their desire to help and be friendly to Filipinos and a need to protect their own integrity. One able and intelligent girl who was passionately dedicated to honesty in her own life asked, "How does one know in a given situation whether a person is deliberately lying or deceiving himself?" Or, she might have added, is it possible that a Filipino is neither deliberately lying nor deceiving himself by saying the words and adopting the rules that would please Americans while acting in ways consistent with his own cultural values.

Volunteers struggled with this issue and constantly asked themselves if they could claim truth, as they understood it, as a universal value which all cultures should respect. Since they had come at the request of the Philippine government, some volunteers could not understand why they had to "play pretend," as one of them put it, in order to achieve the goals of the Peace Corps project. She wrote, "I never compromised so much before in my life, and yet [because she disagreed with her superiors on occasion] I feel like I am being a radical." Most volunteers wanted to accept the persons with whom they were assigned to work, but if acceptance also meant compromising basic principles, their own integrity was assaulted in the process.

Although most volunteers experienced the conflict at some point, they also were capable of resolving it. As one boy described the conflict in the early months, "We were so concerned about being un-ugly Americans, we found ourselves denying our own personalities. We were so careful not to do the wrong things that we made ourselves miserable." For most volunteers the basic problem was distinguishing between accepting persons and values. It was difficult because cultural values and personality are so closely intertwined. But it was sometimes possible to differentiate between major and minor expressions of values that were upsetting. As one girl wrote, "I may not accept all of the values of a particular society, but once I know what those values are, and what is expected of me, I can begin to create my own place, conforming where it is easiest to conform, while retaining those values that are essential to my individual stability." Such a process could mean discovering the core of oneself, the integrity to be protected while admitting an invasion of one's tastes and predilections.

The issue was not precisely the same for any two volunteers. Remaining true to oneself and accepting a school principal or someone else in power who seemed dishonest or obsequious was impossible for some volunteers who perceived him that way. Fortunately, extreme cases were not the rule. It was possible to be accepting and remain true to oneself if acceptance did not lead to paralysis, and if genuineness did not threaten Filipinos in a vital way. It was possible to be honest, yet respectful, courteous, and aware of all the cultural subtleties that keep Americans and Filipinos apart. A volunteer could be true to himself and yet sensitive to every nuance of look and language, particularly those which sent signals of friendship or hostility, which meant so much to Filipinos.

Genuineness without acceptance *could* be terrifyingly frightening to Filipinos who, while often praising Americans for their "frankness," were really deeply hurt by what they experienced as American rudeness. The key to success in the relationship appears to have been the context in which volunteers were genuine. When they exposed their convictions and feelings to Filipinos in the context of caring, even though caring did not mean agreement with values or ideas, Filipinos were less threatened by frank-speaking, achievement-motivated volunteers.[1] The effect in some cases actually was to encourage children and teachers to be more open themselves. One boy, a compulsive worker, dedicated to honesty and ascetic in his habits, who achieved excellent relationships with his coteachers and barrio officials and who appears to have accomplished much good work in his town, told of being at an evening dance with his roommate where he denied a request that he twist. When the record player was turned off at the end of the dance, he asked permission to say a few words:

> You have asked us to come and be with you at this small get-together. We are happy. But we must now come to understand each other. We came here to the Philippines to be with you, to play with you, to work with you, and to live with you. We did not come to be apart from you. But you always insist that we dance alone and apart from you. When I play basketball with your sons, I am not apart. They push and shove me and I do the same . . . [the other volunteer]

[1] Caring *to a Filipino includes being* extremely *careful in sensing the extent to which an honest expression of feelings is hurtful. As is true everywhere, there are culturally approved ways of caring, and, as in most of the world, mere honesty is not one of them. To some Filipinos the previous three chapters of this book by a man who purports to care for them may be considered shameless because of the naked way that American reactions are described.*

and I want to come to your dances. But you need not spend much money or make any great preparations to make us happy. If you simply say, "Come, be with us," we will come and be very happy.

It must now also be made clear that we don't drink *tuba* or beer because we want to be impolite. We don't do it at home. What we do not do at home we will not do elsewhere. If you would have us drink with you, give us a Coke or something similar, and we will come, plain and simple.

Again, we thank you for this evening. We invite you to our house at any time. And please invite us to these dances more often, though possibly not on a school night as we will be able to stay later on a Friday or Saturday. With this understanding, are we all one?

He may have hidden his annoyance or even disgust at being constantly prodded to drink *tuba* and do the twist. Perhaps he was not being completely honest, if honesty is a measure of a complete congruence between feelings and words or actions. But such a standard of honesty seemed irrelevant in the Philippines where sensitive volunteers recognized the importance of not hurting others in a culture where hurting can be totally destructive of communication. As a result of living deeply in Filipino culture, aspects of *pakikisama,* in some cases, had become or were becoming a part of one's own personality. The avoidance of hurtful or hostile feelings was, in such cases, a truer expression of self than their revelation would have been.

Probably the best single way to show one's sincere acceptance of Filipinos was to learn the local dialect. Learning and using the regional or local dialect also gave the volunteers a sense of accomplishment, and made it easier for them to teach the children. While a conscientious, open, and sensitive volunteer who failed to learn the dialect could also have many Filipino friends and be effective in his work, a persistent and successful attempt to study the dialect was an obvious demonstration of a volunteer's concern for people and a key to good communication with them.

Learning the dialect was extremely difficult for many reasons: the volunteer had come to the Philippines to be a model for spoken English in the community as well as the schools and learning the dialect meant continually practicing its use with Filipinos; he received no dialect training in the United States if he was a member of the first seven groups that went to the Philippines; there are six major languages and approximately eighty dialects spoken in the Philippines, which means that it is extremely difficult to produce the materials and to find instructors for the more esoteric tongues (in the Bicol, variations of Bicol are spoken in towns separated by only a few miles); Filipinos would sometimes mimic volunteers or otherwise tease them when they stumbled, and some made invidious comparisons between the slow and the fast learners. (One boy on Leyte who wanted to speak the dialect on every occasion was afraid to be compared unfavorably with two roommates who were superior. "The whole thing led me to want to get away from situations where I would speak and be compared openly . . . I became more silent and talked only when I knew I was right."); and in some towns and barrios Filipinos did not correct volunteers who used the wrong phrase or pronunciation.

Learning the dialect was almost entirely a matter of self-training for the first few groups of volunteers; but many of them persisted. Later the staff and volunteers organized language training programs to collect old and produce new materials for use in special dialect training institutes, because of my conviction that the ability of volunteers to speak in the first language of Filipinos was vital to accepting relationships and to effective work. One boy on the island of Panay wrote that after he became fairly fluent in the dialect, "everything changed. The kids opened up, the elders showed admiration, the market came alive, teaching became meaningful." Increasingly sure in his relationships with Filipinos, he did not mind when they poked fun at his mistakes. "There was no end to the laughter which little slips of accent would pro-

duce. Such were the joys." Another extremely effective volunteer wrote that mastery of the dialect enriched his life in
the Philippines in every way:

> I would stop at the various *sari-sari* stores and visit with
> farmers and storeowners, wrinkled and charming cigar-smok-
> ing matriarchs, game-playing children, and we would talk. In
> a few months, things opened wider and wider. I found I
> could chat with the fishermen about the fish corral, bargain
> with the old vegetable lady, rouse the ashamed child from his
> retreat, sit over a glass of *tuba* with teachers and friends, talk
> of what America was really like, what I was doing in the
> Philippines, about the recent flood, the heat, local evil spirits.
> We sang and laughed and drank in true friendship, joked,
> gossiped. . . .
>
> When I began to feel at home in the second language, I
> was let down from my pedestal. . . . People looked at me
> in a different light. . . . I felt more involved, more an in-
> tegral part of what was going on about me. Things liked
> became more likeable; things annoying became more bear-
> able; relationships more meaningful. In school, the children
> began to draw nearer.

Learning the dialect facilitated mutually accepting relationships which were conducive to mutual change, and the
best way to learn the dialect was to get away from Americans and live with Filipinos. Early Peace Corps plans called
for households of four Americans. In a majority of cases,
these households split up into smaller groups (sometimes as
a result of quarrels), volunteers going off to live alone with
a Filipino helper or to become part of a Filipino family. Although there were exceptions, it became apparent that volunteers who were on their own or with Filipino families tended
to be much more accepting than volunteers who remained in
households with two or three other Americans. Away from
each other, volunteers were obliged not only to discover
more about their barrio neighbors but more about themselves as well. One girl wrote from her remote place, "I have
not seen an American for six weeks now and am enjoying

the Filipinos more than I ever did before. It is too easy to gripe to other Americans about every little thing. If there is no one to gripe to, one just doesn't say anything and everyone is happier for it." Not all volunteers reacted to such extreme isolation with comparable strength and optimism. It probably would be a mistake to let most volunteers live alone in a remote barrio from the first; but most of those who decided to live on their own after careful thought benefited from the change. Nearly every volunteer who decided to move in with a family reported that it was an excellent decision.

ABILITY AND UNDERSTANDING NOT ENOUGH

Without acceptance of Filipinos as persons, the most determined, skilled, and intelligent volunteer was likely to remain frustrated and ineffective in his attempts to change Filipinos in the barrios. Even the much-valued quality of cultural empathy, an intellectual understanding of one's environment, although satisfying to the anthropologically minded volunteer, was no substitute for *pakikisama* in relationships. An extremely bright and sensitive girl who lived on a small, poor island read constantly on the culture and analyzed the behavior of her neighbors. She flung herself into a variety of projects but later wrote that she "plagued myself with too many bright ideas and too many false starts." Despite her sensitive understanding of the culture, she had extreme difficulty in accepting people whose inertia, shame, and what seemed to be hypocrisy threatened her own American standards of integrity and achievement.

One unusually brilliant and capable volunteer tried to introduce a well in the barrio of his small island to improve its drinking water, but, once functioning, the well gave polluted water because the barrio people would not use sanitary toilets. Dedicated to his mission to help Filipinos, he tried other projects. Working in a provincial hospital, he assisted a laboratory technician, who he said refused his suggestions in order to protect her status. Although he tried to show her how to examine stain smears, she refused to learn the procedure because, at least as it appeared to him, she was ashamed of her ignorance.

He also failed in his efforts to inaugurate a water-sealed toilet program, which he planned as a result of a personal study that showed that 99 percent of the 346 children in the barrio school had intestinal parasites. Following the death of one child from an amoebic infection, he obtained a design for cheap, serviceable sanitary toilets and devised a plan for time payments to purchase them. He met with teachers and community leaders who agreed on the need for sanitation. But when he made his proposal, "they said that they were too poor, and didn't have the time required to put up the toilets, and asked me to use my position as an American and as a volunteer to get the government to build them a public toilet."

Another boy, intelligent, skilled, and dedicated, looked back on his mistakes and asked himself, "Why did I make the errors?" His answer was, "Largely because my attention was focused on the project and its demands, not on the people with whom I was working. . . . I was not particularly interested in understanding how other people felt; what I was interested in was getting the job done. As a result, I rode fast and hard, irritating many people in my failure to see that getting the job done was utterly dependent on, and probably less important than, a really clear understanding of the situation in which I was involved."

FALSE DICHOTOMIES

Some volunteers debated the question of the job versus learning or the job versus relationships, although most volunteers were not as distracted by that false issue as officials in Washington or members of my staff in the Philippines. There was no need to speculate on which was more important. The battle between the job and understanding was largely a false one. One could learn more effectively from children and teachers by trying to work with them than by chatting with the boys at the *sari-sari* store or reading books about the Filipino kinship system. Trying to do the job assigned was no barrier to learning; trying to learn from the situation was no obstacle to doing the job. If the Peace Corps teaches the educational establishment in the United States anything about the nature of learning, it is that the most powerful and personally meaningful learnings about human behavior for Americans occur when they are trying to solve difficult human problems in the accomplishment of some task. If the Peace Corps can get that message through to the universities of America, it will have had more impact on the teaching of behavioral sciences than the theoretical writings of John Dewey and the discoveries of learning psychologists.

If the Peace Corps has any meaning for professionals in the field of economic change and development, it is that an approach to working overseas which emphasizes learning through close, personal, accepting relationships is not an obstacle to effecting changes and getting the job done. Indeed, it often may be a necessary precondition for effective change. In my experience, there is no dichotomy most of the time between getting the job done and deep personal learning through caring relationships.

A Peace Corps and technical assistance approach which emphasizes the importance of relationships is no guarantee of effective change in the villages of the world's economically impoverished countries. The unthinking volunteer or technician may use the emphasis on relationships as a substitute for working through the difficult problems of his job or as a rationalization for avoiding the job altogether. Peace Corps planners and staffs overseas may not give sufficient weight to the importance of careful programming and other administrative decisions which will help to facilitate change in the directions desired. But most foreign-aid programs have made the other mistake. They have virtually ignored the importance of human relationships in getting the job done on the false premise that getting the job done was more important than learning about the culture or the language. Dozens of volunteers became hotly critical of the American foreign-aid program in the Philippines and of the failure of AID planners and technicians (with some exceptions) to try to understand Filipinos as persons. They complained that they saw no beneficial results at the local level as a result of foreign aid. They lamented over books locked in libraries, heavy machinery rusting from ill-use, science burners, batteries, and other equipment locked in cabinets that were never opened, pamphlets that were never read, relief clothing that was sold in the market, and—most upsetting of all—AID projects that seemed to have been started without any thought concerning the felt needs and desires of Filipinos. A volunteer from Ilocos Norte complained about an AID project in nutrition. Handsome equipment including large pressure cookers and can sealers were displayed without tarnish or any sign of use in his school. The girl students in home economics were accustomed to a wooden stove, a charcoal hearth, and perhaps a couple of pots at home. The fancy American kitchenware meant nothing to them and never would unless they were motivated to preserve food when it was in season and taught the skills necessary for the task. "Money cannot gain or buy understanding; it takes people and communication," a discouraged volunteer wrote.

From the vantage point of the barrio, it was easy to criticize foreign-aid programs. The lessons of economic development in Western Europe were not transferable to Asian and other poor countries and mistakes were inevitable and understandable. Moreover, there was an inherent disadvantage for AID and its predecessor organizations in promoting economic development when compared to the Peace Corps. Congress had not charged them with the responsibility for learning more about their hosts or with helping Asians, Latin Americans, and Africans to learn more about Americans. It had appropriated billions of dollars in loans, gifts, equipment, and advice on the theory that economic planners and technicians could produce results as they had in the United States and Europe. The professionals recruited to do a job might enjoy some of the quaint customs of the host country, but they were and are not expected to give up the comforts of home. They often live with their families in golden ghettos, and their social life is largely American. In addition, the professional or technician is determined to apply his knowledge in achieving results *on time*. He has reports to make to his superiors and colleagues, and professional standards to uphold. In personal relations he is likely to be *manipulative* in trying to get others to do things the *right* way and *judgmental* when things go *wrong*, the very qualities which Peace Corps volunteers found promotes defensiveness and inhibits fundamental change in others.

Such tactics, Peace Corps volunteers the world over largely agree, have been self-defeating because most of the world does not make the distinction between relationships and the job which is made by Americans and Westerners generally. It is one thing to give economic assistance in Europe with its basic economic infrastructure and where, more importantly, a basic value infrastructure exists for the incorporation of capital, equipment, and skills. But where the basic motivation for economic development remains to be created, a person-centered approach to development appears to be vital.

PROGRAMMING

But a person-centered approach to economic development is not a program. Good Peace Corps programming is necessary not just because it makes volunteers healthier, happier human beings, but because getting the job done—if defined in terms of improving the health, literacy, and physical well-being of Filipinos and others—is important to the hosts. There is only one ultimate test of the validity of American efforts to improve standards of living in the poor countries of the world. It is that when most people experience higher standards of health, literacy, and well-being, they want to keep them despite the painful changes that may accompany them. Asians, Africans, or Latin Americans generally do not prize achievement (or life) as much as Americans, but when they experience health, literacy, and economic well-being, they choose them over disease, illiteracy, and poverty.

Peace Corps planners can develop good programs without necessarily sacrificing the human relations objectives of the Peace Corps. In fact, when such sacrifices are made, programs may be seriously weakened. Good programs depend mainly on the performance of volunteers but also on the administration of overseas staffs and effective planning in the host capitals and Washington. It is not enough to ask the usual questions concerning strategic objectives and available resources or even to assess the needs of a country. Too much planning has been based on some planner's idea of objective needs without attempting to understand which of those needs are felt by the people to be helped. Able Peace Corps volunteers learned eventually how to discriminate between their own version of what was needed in a barrio and the "felt needs" of their neighbors. Good planning also depends upon an accurate assessment of the most effective persons or agencies with whom to work and regions and towns where volunteers should be assigned. This means a judgment as to the willingness to change of some people and agencies against others, the importance of working in towns as opposed to villages or vice versa or in one region as compared to another. Finally, a good Peace Corps program will set limited objectives over time that can be measured against careful research.

THE DEFINITION OF THE TASK

Because of the vagueness of the educational-aide role and the inadequacy of training for it, a major portion of my time and that of my staff went into encouraging the Bureau of

Public Schools to redefine and clarify the role of volunteers, to focus on more specific, realizable objectives, and to help conduct in-service training programs. Because of *pakiki-sama*, it was extremely difficult to obtain the involvement of Filipino officials in the reformulation of program objectives on the basis of their genuine desire and motivation. As long as high officials, as well as barrio principals, looked upon the Peace Corps as just a goodwill program, they could not spell out clear-cut objectives for volunteers. Gradually these officials realized that the talents of volunteers would be wasted considerably unless the role of the educational aide and the goals of the program were sharpened. At my request, the Director of the Bureau of Public Schools appointed a committee of subject-matter experts to investigate the work of the volunteers and to draw up a comprehensive plan for their most effective use. The new project description, completed a year after the first volunteers had reached the field, spelled out a coordinated plan at all public school levels—elementary, high schools, and higher education—in Engish, science, mathematics, and community education.

The major overall objective of the new program was to strengthen teacher training in the Philippines primarily through regular classroom teaching, team teaching, and demonstration teaching in the elementary schools. The project description, which stressed that the best way to teach teachers is by working with children, was no panacea; but it did attack some of the basic job-related problems of volunteers by clarifying relationships with fellow teachers, focusing objectives, and obtaining host-country involvement in planning and supervision.

With the cooperation of the Bureau of Public Schools, the staff also undertook in-service workshops and institutes and the publication of special bulletins and articles to spread information concerning teaching techniques that had already been tried successfully by volunteers and their coteachers. A major step in facilitating workshops was the building of the Peace Corps in-service training center near Zamboanga City on the island of Mindanao, in December, 1962, and in encouraging regional workshops.

THE SELECTION OF COMMUNITIES AND SCHOOLS

Next to giving volunteers support in their attempts to cope with the culture and the non-job, the staff had no more important task than the selection of communities and schools which would give volunteers a chance to make some progress on the job. The selection of communities for the first group of volunteers was made by the Bureau of Public Schools with the cooperation of AID. The basic pattern was to locate volunteers in a relatively large barrio or *poblacion.* The first assignments, determined in Manila before either the volunteers or I arrived in the Philippines, were usually dictated by political factors (*i.e.,* the influence of a provincial superintendent), an attempt to link the volunteers with other aid programs (*i.e.,* assignment in a central school supported by AID funds), and concern for the safety of the volunteer. Probably there was no clear-cut way to identify in advance those schools and communities which would be able to make best use of the volunteers since that kind of information is available only to Americans who have lived in the barrios themselves.

Extreme poverty in a community had a demoralizing effect on some volunteers and tended to limit their confidence and their ability to initiate fundamental change. One volunteer wrote, "It was a full month before we built a functioning toilet (the neighbors did not have one either). We soon learned that the market was good only for fish. Fruit and vegetables had to be sent from M——. Drinking water was fetched further inland and brought to our house by carabao. It cost us about one peso a day for drinking, cooking, and sponge or small dip baths. (The volunteers received 212 pesos a month at that time.) We found our allowance insufficient to cover the cost of food, basic furnishings, postage stamps, and drinking water. We were soon very much in debt." In addition, the volunteer in his household was depressed by the general milieu of the barrio. "The majority of the townspeople make their living by selling the fish they dynamite," he wrote, and "life seemed to be violent . . . [with] many fights, including stabbings."

If a volunteer was in luck or especially sensitive, he might find the individual or group who was ready for what he had to give even in the poorest barrios. One extremely effective volunteer worked in a barrio fourteen kilometers in the mountains at the end of a dead-end road, remote from contact with the flow of commerce and ideas. The economy had been declining because of land abuse; yet, within a year, the barrio leaders were utilizing his help effectively.

No matter how well planning went in Manila or Washington, there were bound to be mistakes in the selection of communities and schools. No matter what the situation, volunteers would be left with the responsibility for defining their goals and locating individuals with status—a principal, barrio lieutenant, vice-mayor, teacher, community development worker, or matriarch—who welcomed what they had to give.

FINDING CO-WORKERS

Beyond an acceptance of *pakikisama,* nothing was more important to the success of the Peace Corps in the Philippines than the ability of volunteers to identify successfully co-workers who could work with them. The identification of what volunteers called "progressive" Filipinos required unusual skill in judging human nature and a great deal of luck.

Occasionally a volunteer's judgment about who was progressive would prove wrong with happy results. One boy was assigned to work with a science teacher who at first stated that he was not interested in teaching science because he lacked equipment, although he actually possessed considerable equipment as a result of Japanese war reparations. He seemed ashamed to admit that he did not know how to use it or to make teaching aids from local materials. Without hope, the volunteer gave his coteacher a science book which told how to construct equipment from native materials for science experiments. The volunteer then turned his attention to teaching English, but when he returned to visit the class of his former coteacher several months later, he found the table filled with science apparatus made from local materials, including balanced scales and a solar system presided over by the happy teacher who even had purchased wiring and batteries from his own salary.

It usually took a long time to locate the forces in a community which were ready for change, and some volunteers believed that they were not able to do so until near the end of their tour of duty. In one of the most successful projects undertaken by volunteers in the first group, a boy and a girl opened a school at the request of barrio leaders during the last six weeks of their service for about eighty out-of-school youths who had no possibility of going to high school.

MAKING A DIFFERENCE

Although most volunteers doubted at some time that they were accomplishing anything, many of them were aware that they could not help but be forces of change in Filipino life. As one of them wrote, "The volunteer is like a small pebble thrown upon a still pool. There is a slight splash and then a continuum of waves generates from this hub. Once the pebble hits the water, a disturbance occurs." Volunteers in the barrio must have seemed strange animals indeed. Filipinos would see them reading, asking questions about what they read, and discussing the answers. Volunteers were generally interested in persons outside their own immediate family. They would try to eat what they called a "balanced diet" and go to a medical doctor when they felt physically ill. They were constantly working to improve their houses, pen chickens, inoculate pigs, and perhaps—strangest of all— they seemed to care zealously about keeping promises, getting to places on time and finishing the job. The peculiar behavior of the *americanos* was bound to affect values as well as institutions, styles, techniques, and habits.[2]

Over the years there had been many examples of Filipino adaptations from Americans, such as the presidential and two-party systems in politics, compulsory education for the young, beauty parlors, basketball, and rock 'n' roll, but these imitations did not seem to affect core values. Volunteers, living deeply in personal relationship, experiencing Filipinos and being experienced by them as persons, undoubtedly did.

But they brooded about it. They knew that in attempting to introduce inductive methods in teaching science, they were trying to have students and teachers think independently in a culture which values dependency in relationships. As they responded to requests for advice on everything from birth control to integrated core curricula and hog breeding, they were plagued sometimes by the ethical implications of the Peace Corps as a venture in cultural imperialism. As one of them put it, "This sort of thing I think about when I'm asked to install electricity in our barrio, or when I am asked to teach a lesson on rockets and satellites by our magic-jewel-carrying, quack-doctor science teacher. . . . I see many things that could be changed from my stateside way of looking at things. I am partial to hi-fi, highways, and higher education, but I can't quite overlook the question; should I?"

The answer was personal, and perhaps many volunteers were never completely satisfied with the one they gave. Others resolved the issue by deciding that life and knowl-

---

[2] *A 336-page study by two social scientists, Thomas W. Moretypi and Frank J. Lynch, S.J., The Philippines Peace Corps Survey Final Report, published by the Social Science Research Institute at the University of Hawaii, confirms this assertion. The Moretypi-Lynch study, done under contract for the Peace Corps and designed to assess the impact of the first nine groups of volunteers in the Philippines, is based on 2,248 interviews of Filipinos in 117 communities that had been served by the Peace Corps and 63 control communities. It revealed changes that included such surprises as a reduction in prejudice against Negroes in communities where volunteers had served. The report shows clearly that volunteers in the first nine groups were also effective in their work in schools, even beyond my own early and naïvely optimistic hopes.*

edge were universally positive values, and that their efforts in the Philippines were basically directed toward enriching the lives and expanding the knowledge of Filipinos. It was also true that there were thousands of Filipinos who consciously wanted the very changes which volunteers were prepared to encourage. Equally true and as important was the fact that change, which had been so slow in coming for centuries, was unquestionably on the way whether the Peace Corps came to the Philippines or not. Surely it was more helpful to Filipinos and others in traditional cultures to have Peace Corps volunteers who respected their traditions and cared about them as people to help in the process of change. Statesmen in the economically poor countries of the world welcomed the volunteers precisely because they were relatively sensitive agents of change. Most volunteers were pleased to be wanted on that basis and happy if they felt they had made a difference.

One of the most accepting and consistently satisfied Peace Corps volunteers looked back at the end of his eighteen months in his barrio to list the things that he thought he left behind: "An approach to science based on exploration and discovery rather than memorization of facts; an approach to English which emphasizes communication rather than rigid rules of grammar and individual style rather than conformity; a class of readers who were formerly nonreaders; a Socratic approach to education; an atmosphere in the classroom which encourages physical, mental, and emotional freedom; an enthusiasm for learning another person's language; an attempt to break down regionalism; a better-trained basketball team; pruned trees around the school; a police dog friendly with strangers; skeletons of hunted birds; a new image of an American; students' laughter; a foster mother; three adopted families; a silent campaign against the tyranny of the powerful; and a multitude of other things, perhaps more important but more difficult to express."

Even when volunteers, as in rare cases, did not feel comfortable at having made changes in the Philippines, the

problem of cultural imperialism in the end was resolved because they became convinced that their personal development—their values, beliefs, and attitudes—had been
changed even more than that of Filipinos. Many volunteers
look back on their experience in the Philippines as a deeply
needed lesson in their own cultural and psychological development and ask not only what is wrong with the Philippines
and how do Filipinos need Americans, but how can Americans enrich their lives as a result of contact with other cultures.

Paradoxically, while volunteers tended to value certain aspects of their Americanness more than ever before, they also
became acutely aware of the loneliness and competitive
struggle which results from valuing independence. They
now cared for people more than they ever had and were
sharply aware of how little caring existed back home. While
many were doubtful that they had done anything to change
Filipinos in fundamental ways, nearly all of them felt deeply
changed themselves.

VI
To experience
each other

: The Peace Corps was a response to the ostensible needs of so-called "developing nations" for better health, education, and greater productivity. But it was also a product of the needs of Americans to live out the ideals of their culture. In the villages of poor countries they hoped to see the fruits of their labor, to make a visible contribution to school and community. As one of them wrote, "I came to the Philippines wanting to *do*, to build, anxious to work with my hands." At the same time, many of them saw the Peace Corps not just as an opportunity to live out the ideals of their culture but to spread them as well. They could, through service in the Peace Corps, not only meet their need for personal achievement but fulfill the national mission to spread the gospel of self-reliance and achievement. That is why conservatives as well as liberals were enthusiastic about the Peace Corps. It not only gave vicarious psychic income to older men and women caught up in the entrails of bureaucratic life (I heard many ambassadors, business executives, and professional men exclaim, "Ah, if only I were young again, that is what I would be doing!") but it also gave a practical expression to Barry Goldwater's hope (in his speech accepting the Republican nomination for the Presidency in 1964) that Americans could "be freedom's missionaries in a doubting world."

But the experience of Peace Corps volunteers revealed an even deeper need than the apparent one which gave birth to the Peace Corps. It was the need to overcome the terrible psychological isolation—the absence of a sense of belonging —which stemmed in large measure from the cult of individualism. At a relatively superficial level, the Peace Corps revealed the need of Americans to live out the ideals of the culture; at a deeper level, it exposed the psychological cost of those ideals and the need of Americans to make up for something their own culture lacked.

Many who joined the Peace Corps already desired, if only subconsciously, opportunities for intimacy and affection that they felt were missing in their own culture. They were ready to be conquered by *pakikisama* even as they went forth to promote individualism and plumbing. In this sense they were quite different from the missionaries of previous times. Not only did they want to respect the otherness of Filipinos; they sensed that there might be something in that otherness that would help them discover more of themselves.

SELF-DISCOVERY

Obviously, generalizations about the meaning of Peace Corps experience are not valid for every volunteer. Throughout this book I have generalized and quantified, using terms like "most," "many," "some," or "nearly all." There were a minority in the first nine groups of Peace Corps volunteers to the

Philippines for whom the rest of this chapter and even much of this book may have little meaning. There were some who did not have a deep personal experience. A few were pleasantly complacent throughout. For others, too many things went wrong; their bitterness was too strong for them to learn much. But most volunteers in the early groups did go through a period of intense and often painful self-discovery. They became aware, as they never had before and probably would not have been able to at home, of aspects of themselves and their Americanness which up to then had been unknown.

Self-discovery resulted partly from the perspective which could be gained away from one's family, friends, and familiar influences. But mainly it was a consequence of struggling with the tensions which grew out of the conflict between the ideals volunteers carried with them to the Philippines and the conflicting values of Filipinos. "I don't believe," wrote one girl from Michigan, "that I have ever gone through a period so frustrating and so full of self-examination in my life, and I don't think I could live through another." Sometimes they were shaken by their discoveries. A girl from Brooklyn wrote, "I feel I've learned some things about life that I might have preferred not to learn . . . at least not now." On their own, not always trusting the reactions of Filipinos, distrusting the reactions of American visitors, and too often without reactions from the staff, volunteers were forced to ever-closer self-examination. A girl from California wrote, "I have been forced, as never before, to know my strengths and weaknesses and to work with them." A New York City girl, struggling with her reactions to Filipinos, began to face what she called "the ugly fact of myself." The growing, acute awareness of self sometimes led to a lowering of defenses—"I am now able to look at myself in the harsh light of reality," said a boy from New Jersey.

A minority were shaken by their inability to crash through the various cultural barriers that faced them in the non-job and in the community, but most of them gained strength from having had the burden of individual responsibility for making a life and a job for themselves. Self-confidence took quantum jumps for many. "I have learned to accept and handle the responsibility of planning, carrying out and judging my own work with no one to wave incentives before me." Many expressed appreciation for the opportunity, as a girl from Oregon put it, "to trust my own judgment." An Iowan felt that because he was forced to try a variety of things and succeeded at some of them, his self-confidence mushroomed. A girl from Tennessee exclaimed, "I have had more responsibility than I perhaps will ever have again. . . . How often at home would I have been asked to introduce a governor on a program or speak before a civic club or to help a mayor on a project? How often will teachers at home more experienced than I listen to advice from me or even ask for it?" A California boy wrote that because he had the opportunity to work out problems for himself while he was in the Peace Corps, he "gained terrific confidence in myself . . . I don't think anything is impossible." A boy from Brooklyn who once doubted his ability to stick it through in the Peace Corps was astounded by his growing belief "not only in my ability to do a tough job, but to do it happily."

THE COMPLEXITY OF DISCOVERY

Growing self-confidence did not preclude a growing sense of uncertainty about how one would fit in American life or a keener appreciation of one's weaknesses and inconsistencies. Peace Corps volunteers proved that the most significant learnings were rarely one-sided or simple. Every discovery, it seemed, had its opposite accompanying it.

Living in a culture of poverty, many volunteers became more thankful that they had been born to a land of plenty and more aware of the misery and malnutrition and disease which poverty brings. They became more determined to eliminate inequality, too. A girl from Ohio wrote that she couldn't help "but hate the idea that some have so very much" after she lived "among so many poor where there is no rice for supper, where the children have no pencils for school, where their clothes are in tatters." But many volunteers began to understand the poverty of riches, too. A wealthy girl from Indiana saw a "naturalness of the barrio" which she compared to the "falsity of the rich."

The Peace Corps experience led to many kinds of impatience. Volunteers became impatient with social injustice and bureaucracy. A girl from Georgia who had been brought up to believe in segregationist ideas turned on them sharply in the Peace Corps, where some of her friends were Negroes and where "there are, of course, all the wonderful Filipinos with whom I lived and worked." Many talked impatiently about the bureaucratization of education. They scoffed at "Mickey-Mouse courses" in colleges back home. But sometimes the same volunteers were aware of having become more patient than they had ever been in their lives. A Negro boy from Ohio wrote that he no longer expected results tomorrow or next year in working on social problems. He gained more courage to face the race problem back home, but he felt more patient, too.

Most volunteers became much more aware of nature than they ever had before. If they lived in the eastern Visayas, they knew the fearful, destructive power of typhoons. In much of the Philippines they choked in the hot, parched earth of the dry season and longed for a patch of blue when the rains came. But at the same time, many of them became more aware of what a boy from Washington D.C. saw as "the textures and colors and steaming fertility of the Philippines." At the end of his work in the barrios, he wrote that the plants of the Philippines excited him as much as they did on his arrival. A girl from a small town in Illinois wrote to me from her nipa house that "the beauty for me is almost overwhelming." At night she lighted fires from palms that fell from the coconut tree during the day and watched the flames against the sunset. Another girl, this one from Wisconsin, wrote that she had developed "an almost sensual

awareness of love for nature . . . I think I have found
something in the sea and the mountains that is almost like
having a lover. I delight in it, revel in it, love it." For many
there was a new awareness of a different way of relating to
nature. Not by conquering or controlling it but by blending
into it. A girl from a suburb of New York City saw more
unity in nature than ever before. When she saw a Filipino
whom she knew climb a coconut tree or put up the sail of a
vinta and head into the wind, she viewed him as: "an inte-
gral part of the natural world. Seeing an American do the
same thing might make me feel that he is imposing upon
nature . . . but R. [the Filipino] belongs, he is part of the
tree, a part of the sea. Seeing him catch and ride a horse is
to see a fragment of the mythical times when man and horse
were one."

UNDERSTANDING AMERICANNESS

Volunteers saw themselves and nature in new ways, and
they also developed a new angle of vision for understanding
the culture and society from which they sprang. "I have
been able to see myself as an American interacting and reacting to another culture. I never realized to what an extent
I was an American, carrying like genes the values, attitudes
[and] beliefs of Western civilization. Sometimes I felt like a
mechanical toy performing functions that had no meaning,"
wrote one boy.

Many volunteers developed a considerable pride in the
organizational ability and efficiency of Americans. They
could understand more clearly how entrepreneurial and organizational talents led to great power and wealth which
made democracy possible. Yet at the same time they became, as one boy from Iowa said, "more patient with inefficiency." It was impossible to live nearly two years in a
bahala na culture, make friends whom one enjoyed and
loved, without being affected by *bahala na. Bahala na* had
many expressions. For a boy from Kentucky, it was a realiza-

tion that "not all of life can be put into getting the most for your time or money. Nor can everything be explained or analyzed. Fate," he concluded, "does play a part." A girl from Oregon wrote that she liked her new sense of time. In the United States time controlled her. "Here," she wrote, "it ebbs and flows like the tide." A California boy found that he had learned "not to take offense at things I would have ordinarily considered offensive. I've been tested so many times on my sensitivity that it has almost become a game. You might say that I could be an illustration for a cartoon captioned 'Nothing bothers me anymore.'" Commented a girl from a small town in upstate New York, "I have learned to relax. I have learned to accept things as they come." Conversations that used to seem meaningless to her now held her interest. At any rate, when she was bored or annoyed, she could say, *"Bahala na."*

A girl from another small town in New York State who had had many frustrations on the job concluded before she went home that she had learned to be more easygoing. Things which she used to worry about "do not upset me or even seem important." An Ohio girl found that *bahala na* made her more "tolerant of dirt, inefficiency . . . to the point where I'm not fully aware that they even exist. . . . I no longer feel irritated when the neighbors' chickens fly over my fence and bother my penned chickens or when the flies come from his open toilet to my dinner plate." *Bahala na* had its attractions, and many volunteers realized that Americans were frenetic and harried consumers of time. But rarely did they find a sense of completion and frequently they missed a sense of harmony with nature, others, and themselves.

The one aspect of Americanness which most volunteers seemed to like more than ever before was its emphasis on opportunity for the individual for whatever self-expression was desired regardless of race, color, sex, or creed. One girl from New York City, admitting that there were many things she did not admire in her own culture, proclaimed, "I am glad to be an American woman and not a Filipina. I appreciate our opportunity to rise in the world." A girl from Maryland saw more clearly that "America *is* a land of opportunity." A small-town New Jersey girl wrote that after having lived in the midst "of real inequality in a society with little social mobility, . . . it makes me glad I'm an American." In the Philippines, she wrote, a boy of the barrio might be a genius, but if he had no money or influence, it was virtually impossible to get a higher education. A Negro girl who had grown up in a slum outside Portland, Oregon, wrote, "I believe more strongly in the basic tenets of democracy, and particularly in the pioneer spirit of America. I do not think that a system that infringes on an individual's initiative is in any way desirable." Another Negro girl, this one from Maryland, wrote that "life here has made me love and appreciate America as never before."

But the growing appreciation of opportunity for the individual, like the growing appreciation of efficiency and order, was accompanied by a clearer recognition that the cult of individualism and self-sufficiency had somehow separated Americans from each other. By making personal independence and achievement the supreme values of life, many Americans had cut themselves off from the loving, mutual relationships which volunteers experienced in Filipino families and with Filipino friends. Whereas Americans had made independence from and within relationships an important ideal, Filipinos, through *pakikisama,* valued mutuality in relationships more than anything. As was true of *bahala na,* there were aspects of *pakikisama* that repelled the volunteers. But also as with *bahala na,* there were qualities of *pakikisama* that made them acutely aware of their own psychological needs as Americans.

While volunteers found that the system of *utang na loob* often was upsetting, many of them concluded, as a boy from California said, that "strangely enough I'm going to carry something of this system home with me." The personalization of life in the Philippines penetrated the reserve of volunteers, one of whom, a boy from a small town in Florida wrote that he was delighted to discover "the genuine pleasure that can be found in association with people." Another boy from California who had earlier prided himself on his tough-minded independence concluded that "the major source of gratification during my service in the Peace Corps has been the friendships I have made in the Philippines." A girl from Pennsylvania who complained frequently about the staff and the problems of the culture wrote that while she had seen more hurt and suffering than ever before, she had become more involved in happiness and love too.

Despite themselves, volunteers were caught in the web of *utang na loob* and the pleasures of *pakikisama*. As soon as they accepted Filipinos as persons, they were able to enjoy the smiles, jokes, and small talk of their hosts. Dozens of them agreed with the boy who wrote that "some of the most pleasant times I've had were just sitting in the *sari-sari* store and talking with groups of people." Typical was the comment of a rugged boy from Texas, who wrote: "The other day a man from the barrio greeted me on the road with a big smile and 'Happy afternoon.'. . . It was an inspiration to look up and see him and then to count my blessings following that small but significant greeting."

CARING RELATIONSHIPS

The mutuality in relationships of Filipino families and friends flowed easily. Filipinos were dependent on each other. They knew and accepted that fact and loved each other because of it. As time passed, volunteers were drawn to those qualities of sharing and loving while still rejecting many of those aspects of *utang na loob* which seemed to squelch social and economic opportunity for individuals. They appreciated the gracious gifts given to them by small children and poor neighbors who could barely afford them. They loved to watch the students for whom they had provided scholarships, because they were "their children." Four girls who sponsored sixteen children in a high school wrote that "we even think of these high school children as our own in some ways and have become very involved in their family and school situations." Wrote a Minnesota boy, "My work with the children in my school has been the most rewarding experience of my life. In these children's faces of smiles and shining eyes, I become aware of the brotherhood of man." A Virginia boy who at first had many negative reactions to the Philippines and Filipinos discovered a new capacity in himself to relate to people and enjoy the ebb and flow of life and was amazed at himself. "There are picnics, jam sessions, parties . . . and then many evenings when we just sit around and talk," he wrote in explaining what the Peace Corps had meant to him.

Volunteers were learning to care in relationships in a way that involved, committed, and obligated them. They were caring as Filipinos cared. They discovered, as a Massachusetts boy put it, "the value of a warm exchange of unhurried greetings; of a concern for another's being; of happiness in playing or singing." A New York girl wrote: "I found the greatest pleasure in living in the barrio, getting to know the people, sharing their joys and sorrows—their life. To the best of my ability I became a part of that life and was happiest when I could do so. To make friends and be accepted by them overshadowed any minor frustrations." She attended a fiesta in another town with one of the teachers from her school whose family lived in the town. When she was introduced to the family, she faced all the usual questions: Did she eat rice? Did she know how to say thank you in the dialect? and so on. Her coteacher, now a good friend, burst out laughing. Of course the *americana* ate rice and many other things, the Filipina said. Not only could she say thank you, but she could carry on a conversation in the dialect. "It was," the volunteer wrote, "as if she and I shared a secret. We knew each other, we understood each other; we were friends."

A Wisconsin girl described the process of opening oneself

to *utang na loob* and *pakikisama.* She said that after learning the dialect, her fear of participating in situations over
which she had no control was reduced. "I would make a
commitment to attend a party or visit a particular place
without being sure when I would be asked the same questions. . . . I became less defensive and more willing to accept whatever happened to me. . . . Soon it wasn't an
effort. I often anticipated rather than dreaded participation."

Simple talks led to rich friendships. An Indiana boy told
of a beautiful night "when several of the teachers and I
walked through the streets, the moon poking through the
coconut shadows on our way to the sea where we sat on the
wharf talking and enjoying each other. Our voices were soft
. . . we didn't talk about peace, war, English, science, or
any of the important concerns of great men. We talked
about things so simple as not to be remembered. . . . I
went to bed with a smile, a contentment." He wrote also of
the nights when he and several of the men teachers worked
together to make toilet bowls, and how he enjoyed the questions that they asked about America and Americans. "After a
fifth of brandy and four hours of chatter, T. would wake up
the store owner and buy a pint of brandy, four Pepsis, and a
can of spam . . . We talked some more and finally the
teachers walked me home because they did not want the
dogs to bite me and it would have been inhospitable to let
me go home alone. Later I took great pleasure at being able
to walk some of these men home and leave them at their
door."

Such unhurried moments of human contact and sensitivity
touched many volunteers deeply. Such moments had been
rare in impersonalized America and many volunteers freely
acknowledged that they had never experienced them quite
like that before. Friendships were fed by caring and love. As
a girl from Wisconsin wrote of a friend in the school system,
"She knows that she can hold my hand in public on the
streets without causing me embarrassment; she knows that I

would rather meet her friends and family than eat in an American restaurant. I love her, and she knows that." An Illinois girl admitted that "I had never been such a loving person before."

CARING MEANS INVOLVEMENT

Many volunteers became aware that caring, loving relationships meant becoming involved. The detachment which seemed so closely related to the highly prized value of personal independence fell before the pleasures of *pakikisama*. A Wisconsin boy remembered how, when at college, a close friend woke him at three in the morning to share a problem. They talked for several hours and he listened, "but refused to become intimately involved. In the morning, I concluded that the meaningful cannot be shared." But in the Philippines, his experience taught him the joy of personal involvement. "You do not lose yourself in involvement; the contrary is closer to my experience," he wrote. He learned in the Philippines that the self which he had always sought could never be caught and could never really be expressed except through relationships with others.

Another volunteer, a boy from New Hampshire, said, "I used to think that I could take people or leave them. They are more important now, or maybe just more of a feeling of I do this for you rather than I do this for you for me." It was another way of saying *basta ikaw*. A New York City girl summed it up, "I have become so much more aware of basic humanness . . . unafraid of humanness . . . profoundly and painfully aware that the only things worthwhile in life are sincere relationships with other human beings. . . . It was a beautiful thing to me to see the close family ties . . . a sort of unafraid admission of the need of one for another; and more than the feeling, the unashamed acting out of the feeling."

Here was a discovery that Americans could be shamed too. They could be shamed by revealing feelings of dependency, of needing others, by betraying their inability to achieve the self-sufficiency exalted by the culture. Volunteers looked at Filipino families which were vastly different from those they had known. A girl from Ohio was amazed that she had to travel halfway around the world to find out what close family relationship could mean. She wrote, "I liked becoming part of a family and doing the things they did." Another volunteer, a girl from upstate New York who had been adopted by a Filipino family, including a 76-year-old grandfather who spoke no English and referred to her as his daughter, wrote, "I will always think of them as my family." A girl from Rhode Island who had prized her independence highly wrote of "an entire family who opened their hearts to me. I was loved and loved each one in return. Because I loved and valued them, I learned to appreciate those unspoken values by which they lived; I felt the value and the goodness and the rightness of the kinship system, of 'face,' and other values. . . . I can understand why people will resist changing these patterns because the goodness of them will disappear with the bad."

The importance of family, *compadres* and *comadres*, godfathers and godmothers, was constantly impressed upon volunteers. One girl wrote that she was thrilled to be asked to be the godmother of a newly born baby, even though—as a Protestant—the priest would not let her assume that role. She wrote, "Last Sunday I was quite excited to stand up in front of the church, even if only as a witness. Though he is in truth not my godchild, the feeling I have with him and his family is a very special one. I know that I can always depend on them and they feel the same way about me, . . . always available to help, reliable, full of love and warmth." A boy from South Carolina who extended his service in the Peace Corps for a third year wrote at the end of that year that he felt able to be part of the lives of his Filipino neighbors "as they do things with each other and me." He now felt able to relate to Filipinos freely without being torn or threatened by unfamiliarity "and the desperate need to com-

municate. I was whole and the bonds and patterns of communications were whole." He concluded, "The important
idea to me is mutualness." A girl from Indiana wrote, "I
think most of us have learned to soften our concept of
rugged individualism as we have come to realize we do need
others."

Volunteers developed a sense of love and loyalty to individuals, families, and what they called "my place." Even
when it would have been best for them and their work to
move, it was difficult to make a transfer because of the
affection they had developed for the children and their
neighbors. A girl who was miserable because of the corruption and opposition of local school officials wrote, "I feel loyalty to this place and want to help here. I feel this is my
home now." A volunteer became accustomed to his market,
his *sari-sari* store, his neighbors and friends.

The feeling was not a patronizing concern for "my village."
It was a sense of belonging. It was a feeling of attachment
and involvement which made a volunteer from a city in upstate New York express amazement that "people with such
different backgrounds could actually come to understand
each other deeply and love each other as human brothers."
Yet they did. Despite the conflicts, frustrations, and even
bitterness, volunteers learned to care for other persons perhaps more deeply and sensitively than most Americans ever
do in a lifetime. Wrote one boy, "Whenever I read or hear
about the Philippines . . . it will be like hearing about relatives and friends. I am as concerned about what goes on
here as I am with what goes on at home because I identify
with the people . . . their problems are mine." A boy from
Massachusetts who had always thought of himself as being
idealistic, concluded his service in the Philippines feeling: "I
know far more about caring, am far more aware of the
worth and importance of that marvelous word than I ever
was before." At the same time that volunteers became more
aware of the relativity of cultural values and more appreci-
ative of certain aspects of their Americanness, they also be-

came more understanding of the universalities in human nature. Vague phrases such as "world community" and "the
brotherhood of man" acquired specific, personal meanings in
close, warm friendships.

INDIVIDUALISM ABROAD

What makes Peace Corps volunteers peculiar *among* Americans is not that they exemplify the dominant values of the
culture, but that they have questioned those values and have
seen beyond them. Other Americans who live abroad—tourists, scholars, missionaries, businessmen, diplomats, and the
military—tend to reveal the same dominant values of personal independence and achievement shown by Peace Corps
volunteers, although perhaps not to the same degree. Wherever Americans go and in whatever capacity, they take their
values with them, and they are seen as peculiar by their
hosts. As colonial administrators in the Philippines, Hawaii,
and Puerto Rico, as proconsuls in defeated Germany and
Japan following World War II, and as technical assistants in
the capitals of the economically impoverished countries,
they preach the virtues of self-sufficiency (the capacity to
act independently).

Wherever Americans have gone, they have been surprised
and disappointed to find that others did not value individualism. For all the other great cultures of the world, including the peasant cultures of Europe, it is the group, not the
individual, which is important. Whether the group is a family, clan, or village, harmony and cohesion are valued, not
personal independence. Only in the West, and especially in
the United States, has the assertion of the independent self
been the dominant response to man's quest for identity. In
the Pacific Islands, Asia, Latin America, Africa, and even in
the cultures of Europe where a self apart from the group
is unthinkable, American individualism is seen as peculiar.

In most of the world people answer the question, Who are
you? by saying I am of X village or of Y family. Nearly

everywhere there is some variant of *utang na loob,* with its emphasis on fixed reciprocity of obligation among unequals. Status is prescribed; authority and tradition are the appropriate guides for decision; relationships are not fragmented but total within the circle of the family or clan; and frank and direct confrontation is usually avoided in order not to disrupt the harmony of the group. For the majority of the people of the world, the individual grows up through an unending series of dependency relationships within a large kinship circle. Marriage does not signify the development of a fully independent unit but marks the beginning of a new set of relationships which are governed by reciprocity and inherited status. What most Americans would see as unwanted dependency feelings are viewed favorably. In India, for example, where there is no word for dependency, the terms *bandha, sambandha,* and *bandhavy* (bond, bondship, and kinship) have a positive connotation. An Indian, like a Filipino, who asks a favor of someone of higher status, even on a short acquaintance, is expressing his hope for closeness and bondship and is willing to obligate himself in appropriate ways in return for the favor.

Life in most of the world is personalized. A Filipino sitting in a group discussion may not be able to tell you the content of the discussion, but he may be able to interpret with sensitive detail the feelings of friendliness or hostility of every member of the group. The ideal of human maturity is not independence from and within relationships but in satisfying, pleasurable, and continuous dependency relationships.

From the point of view of most people in the world, the American emphasis on achievement is as peculiar as the American stress on independence. Nearly everywhere there is some equivalent of *bahala na.* Almost every major language of Asia has as one of its most common phrases its own *bahala na.* Most of the people of the world see no great virtue in work, punctuality, efficiency, and planning. One may work hard but not necessarily earn more. One may earn more but still eat less. Others are not driven with engines to speed them from task to task or with cognitive maps which purport to explain all phenomena in order to subdue and control the natural world in man's behalf.

Whereas Americans have tended to see most other people as slaves to authoritarian and group controls and as pessimistic and fatalistic, immigrants to this country and foreign visitors or students from the eighteenth century to the mid-1960's have seen Americans as distinguished by their emphasis on independence in relationships aimed at personal achievement. Personality traits which are mentioned most frequently by foreigners include self-reliant (to be able to choose on one's own, one must know how to choose); active (when status is no longer prescriptive, it must be won by ceaseless labor); empirical (when authority and tradition are eliminated as guides for behavior and reason, experience takes their place); gregarious and conformist (when men are psychologically on their own and physically mobile too, they seek the superficial fellowship of others outside the family circle partly to find out how they are doing and partly to discover what others are doing so as to adopt the latest fashion or mode); frank (when men are judged by qualities of independence, they feel a compulsion to express disagreement with authority and tradition); naïve and optimistic (when men are confident of the possibilities of change through personal choice and achievement, they are hopeful about the future and unmindful of complexities and difficulties). Dozens of the latest accounts of students, tourists, and journalists point to the continuing peculiar American emphasis on independence, social equality, and achievement.[1]

[1] *Seymour Martin Lipset's brilliant book,* The First New Nation *(Basic Books, Inc., New York, 1963), persuasively argues the importance of continuity in American values. He sees the values of equality and achievement as preeminent. What he calls equality is closely related to my concept of independence. It is a kind of social equality which implies an equality of opportunity. It is not, of course, equality of condition. It seems to me that the capacity and the right to make choices without restraint get somewhat closer to the deepest value of the culture than social equality itself, which is a concomitant of independence.*

THE PSYCHOLOGICAL COST

Nearly all foreigners have commented on what they have seen as "excessive individualism." The most astute observer of them all, Alexis de Tocqueville, wrote: "In most of the operations of the mind each American appeals only to the individual effort of his own understanding." Another important related theme widely held by foreign observers is the anxiety of Americans. Two sources of anxiety are commonly referred to. Americans are seen as being extremely anxious about success and about belonging. Concern over success comes from the very high value which Americans place on personal achievement, getting from here to there, climbing the ladder, running the race. Concern over belonging comes from the value which Americans place on independence from and within relationships, not getting tied down, being free to make one's own decisions, and being mobile.

De Tocqueville understood both forces of anxiety and he was discouraged to see the effects. "In America," he wrote, "I saw the freest and most enlightened men placed in the happiest circumstances the world affords; [yet] it seemed to me as if a cloud hung upon their brow and I thought them serious and almost sad, even in their pleasures." The German economist and sociologist, Werner Sombart, saw anxiety in America as stemming from the fact that "since all are seeking success. . . everyone is forced into a struggle to beat every other individual; and the steeplechase begins . . . that differs from all other races in that the goal is not fixed, but constantly moves even further away from the runners." Even in play, many observers noticed, Americans seemed a driven, careworn people. Independence was not guaranteed by financial security at birth. In fact, inherited wealth made it more difficult for some to demonstrate their self-sufficiency in moral and emotional terms. Ability or worth was not meas-

---

Most of Lipset's argument and the abundant evidence he cites could be used equally well to support the idea of a continuity in the preeminent values of personal independence and achievement.

ured merely in terms of money but primarily in terms of how much money one could earn *on one's own* without too much of a headstart.

Europeans found Americans assertive and aggressive and on the surface self-confident, but the most perceptive of them saw an underlying anxiety which betrayed the surface confidence. Even the vaunted American optimism—boosterism and self-congratulation—was a way of convincing oneself as well as others that success, if not already here, was just around the corner.

The gregarious and conformist tendencies in American culture also betray a considerable amount of anxiety. The cult of self-sufficiency, making extraordinary demands on the individual, cannot help but lead to what James Bryce saw as a tendency to fall in line with the dominant opinion. For the tyranny of the family, church, or tribal leaders, Americans substituted what de Tocqueville called the tyranny of the majority. For more than 150 years Americans have anxiously looked for signs of majority opinion in cliques, clubs, associations, or public opinion polls. It is important to know not just what the opinion is today, but what it will be tomorrow. The tyranny of being up to date and fashionable, it would seem, has been America's special brand of slavery. Francis Grund in *Aristocracy in America* remarked in the 1830's that "nothing can excite the contempt of an educated European more than the continual fears and apprehensions in which even the 'most enlightened citizens' of the United States seem to live with regard to their next neighbors, lest their actions, principles, opinions and beliefs should be condemned by their fellow creatures."

Not feeling close ties of belonging to family, clan, tribe, or even church, most middle-class Americans (particularly Protestants) have desperately tried to belong to something. De Tocqueville saw that "the same equality that renders him [the American] independent of each to his fellow citizens, taken severally, exposes him alone and unprotected." Here was a culture—the first in human history—where an ever-

increasing number of people drew little psychological satisfaction and strength from being able to say, "I am a
woman"; "I am a mother"; "I am a man"; "I am a father"; "I
am the son of L"; "My grandfather is of the House of ——"; "I
am a shoemaker"; "My ancestors were teachers"; and on and
on. Here it was necessary for man to show that he could
accomplish tasks on his own which were approved in the
market of public opinion. The result was a feeling of being
alone which individuals in caste or class or family or village-
dominated societies probably have never known. De
Tocqueville described the psychological consequences of
self-sufficiency when he wrote of Americans:

> They owe nothing to any man, they expect nothing from
> any man; they acquire the habit of always considering them-
> selves as standing alone, and they are apt to imagine that
> their whole destiny is in their hands. Thus not only does
> democracy make every man forget his ancestors, but it hides
> his descendants and separates his contemporaries from him;
> it throws him back forever upon himself alone and threatens
> in the end to confine him entirely within the solitude of his
> own heart.

ADAM AND ATOM

The psychological isolation which de Tocqueville and others
described was Adamistic at its source and atomistic in its
manifestations. The prophets of American values, from
Jefferson to Emerson and Thoreau, to William James and
John Dewey, have insisted that the individual should trust
no one but himself. The ideal man is ready to confront the
challenges of life dependent only on his unique abilities. He
lives and achieves apart from his historical and cultural inheritance. Emerson, whose influence on American education, philosophy, and psychology has probably been larger
than that of any other American, never tired of urging the
individual, "Trust thyself . . . nothing is at last sacred but
the integrity of your own mind; . . . the only right is what

is after my constitution; the only wrong is against it." Man, wrote Emerson, should "scorn to imitate any being, let him scorn to be a secondary man, let him trust fully to his own share of God's goodness . . . it will lead him on to perfection which has no type yet in the universe, save only in the Divine Mind."

Emerson never asked how man learned to trust himself (if not through being trusted and loved by others) or how he developed his own voice or manner. Not only is every man unique (a banality on which all could agree) but he has presumably sprung full-blown from the head of Zeus. His inner self apparently has little to do with family or history. Emerson was reacting to the incredibly powerful Puritan controls of his immediate ancestors and to the American environment which encouraged the disintegration of Puritanism when he asked, "Cannot we let people be themselves, and enjoy life in their own way? You are trying to make that man another *you*. One's enough." Here was the cult of the individual stated as purely as it had ever been before. "No law can be sacred to me but that of my nature," said Emerson. The sins of Christian morality were expunged. "Sin," wrote Emerson, "is when a man trifles with himself and is untrue to his own constitution."

INDIVIDUALISM IN FAMILIES

The widespread belief in the absolute value of self-reliance has made Americans atomistic in their anxiety over restraints of any kind, including those which come from any close, mutually dependent social and family relationships. The self-sufficiency required to make choices on one's own has required freedom from continuing entanglements with others. Few have dared to follow Emerson's exhortation, "Let us feel if we will the absolute insulation of man . . . let us even bid our dearest friends farewell, and defy them, saying 'Who are you? Unhand me: I will be dependent no more,' " but millions have envied and honored the ideal of being free from prescriptive obligations of any kind, even to friends, parents, and spouses.

Emerson has been foremost among the priests of American individualism, but he has had a great deal of company. Poets and writers have repeatedly described and exemplified the psychological consequences of the dispersive, centrifugal forces inherent in the cult of individualism.[2] Rarely would a public man—politician or businessman—whose pseudo-strength comes from popularity acknowledge the psychic toll taken in a culture which makes its highest values personal independence and achievement. *Many* superficial relationships (one can pretend they're enjoyable; at least they may lead to votes or more business) are unthreatening; but close relationships which imply continuing obligation, particularly in families, are.

By the late nineteenth century, most middle-class American families were highly atomized. The shrewd French observer, Paul Bourget, wrote of the families he saw in American resort hotels that "the members of these families live side by side rather than with one another." He went on, "The American family appears to be more than anything else an association, a sort of social camp, the ties of which are more or less strong according to individual sympathies such as might exist between people not of the same blood." It occurred to him that the relationships between siblings, father and son, and mother and daughter were "entirely elective."

The family, which earlier had been portrayed as a safe retreat and haven for competitive man, was seen increasingly in the literature of America as a prison. In the mind's eye, childhood had been idyllic (see Whittier's "Barefoot Boy"), but the tensions of adolescence and the responsibilities of marriage and parenthood were increasingly stressful in a culture which idealized the assertion of self regardless of age, sex, or role. The child at least had his mother's knee and

---

[2] *I am particularly indebted to Professor William Bridges of Mills College for enlarging my understanding of the relationships of American poetry to American character.*

the promises of tomorrow. The grown man had his failures, and when successful, the fear of failure. Even when successful without fear of failure, to judge from literature of the late nineteenth and early twentieth centuries, he rarely had a firm sense of belonging.

Americans were cursed with the cultural injunction: Go it alone! What could be more frightening to children than to say, You are on your own. To judge first from fictional and now from psychological literature, the central source of anguish for Americans became the feeling of not being cared for, wanted, of not belonging. How was it possible to go it alone and give and receive love? How was it possible to be independent and feel the mutuality of warm, giving relationships with others? The ideology of independence thrived under the impact of technology and urbanization and the diffusion of abundance. It became something that middle-class women and children could afford as well as men. As the cold war between generations, among siblings, and between spouses replaced the family circle of the early nineteenth century, Americans increasingly sought outside of families an answer to their need for belonging.

THE NEED TO BELONG

One answer was the utopian communities which sprang up in the 1830's and 1840's. The communal family was seen as one way to avoid the possessiveness and problems of authority and obligation that go with having children in a limited family circle. To avoid the possessiveness and obligations that go with monogamy, some thought it best to share even marriage and sexual love among many spouses. If one could break the nuclear family, it might be possible to free everyone from the ties which bind and yet give all a sense of purposeful belonging and sharing.

Another response was through religion, particularly through the evangelical revivals of fundamentalist Protestantism. One could at least belong to God; and at the church supper, and especially at the revival meeting, one could feel the communion of one's fellow man, however fleeting. To sing out together, to share one's feelings in ecstasy and hope, released hundreds of thousands from the solitude of their own hearts. In the camp meeting or the revival hall, fundamentalist Protestants could make a perfect marriage of the ideology of independence and the craving of individuals for human contact. The fundamentalists, more than those in the high churches, emphasized the individual's lonely encounter with God but did it through mass singing, dancing, and shouting.

The most common answer of Americans to reconciling the need to remain independent and the need to belong has been to form clubs, organizations, and associations of all kinds. From the early nineteenth century on, we have been a nation of joiners. As Will Rogers once quipped, "Americans will join anything but their own families." In associations one might accomplish something too, even achieve a little recognition. There are presidencies, vice-presidencies, and other offices to win, in addition to accomplishing the objectives of the group. But regardless of recognition or achievement, there is the gratification of belonging. Whether at church socials, garden clubs, civic clubs, or American Legion meetings, there is the camaraderie and fellowship of contact with other human beings. The relationships are tenuous and superficial, but because of that, they are not binding.

Emerson would have none of these answers, neither utopian societies, religious revivals, nor associational life. He saw love between persons as largely a delusion. To achieve a sense of belonging, man had to change his orientation from society with its forces of internal division to nature with its forces of integration. Only then could man liberate and understand himself. But this was no Buddhist annihilation of self, no merging of self with nature. The self remained very much aware of its separateness. There is a circularity in Emerson's thought. The way to be separate and happy is to let other persons be separate too. Why that guarantees happiness and how that makes up for the desire to belong is not made clear. Emerson's way of defending his own extreme shyness in relationships with others was to elevate the qualities of self-sufficiency and separateness to moral virtues and to seek refuge in nature.

Walt Whitman, who liked to think of Emerson as his mentor (as have hundreds of highly influential Americans), was also leery of affectional—especially familial—bonds. He saw families as expedients, since the whole world could not live under one roof. But in his scale of society there were only two units that really mattered: the individual and the mass. Any group in between was extraneous or threatening because it was controlling. But unlike Emerson, Whitman acknowledged his craving for human relationships. In his poetry he sees the restoration of self through love, but his love relationships are fleeting, transitory, and thus not binding in any way. His call goes out to all:

> O that you and I escape from the rest and
>   go utterly off, free and lawless,
> Two hawks in the air, two fishes
>   swimming in the sea
>   not more lawless than we.

Families were nothing special to Whitman, who showed a definite preference for the passing stranger. Belonging to families, after all, cuts down one's independence. He wrote that his love would pick him out by secret and divine signs, "acknowledging none else, not parent, wife, husband, brother, child any nearer than I am." He went on, "Some are baffled, but that one is not—that one knows me." One could not afford to be known in a highly competitive, individualistic society; but everyone desperately needed to be known, at least by one other. If the other could be a stranger, so much the better. Whitman wrote, "Passing Stranger! you do not know how longingly I look upon you, you must be he I was seeking, or she I was seeking." Feeling his loneliness, aware that others must feel theirs, he thought of other men "yearning and thoughtful," and realized that "if I could know these men I should become attached to them."

Even more than did Emerson, Whitman apparently knew the terrifying side of separateness. He wrote of "a noiseless patient spider" who "stood isolated" and "launch'd forth filaments, filaments, filaments, out of itself" until "the gossamer threads you fling catch somewhere, O my soul." In an earlier version of the same poem, Whitman saw the soul as "reaching, throwing out for love," as the spider threw out filament after filament "that one at least may catch and form a link, a bridge, a connection." Whitman wanted the connection, like all Americans, but not relationships which would inhibit his independence. He had a great hatred for the very idea of dependency, and like Emerson, he saw the child as *tabula rasa* without family or group controls of any kind. In the first five sections of *Song of Myself* he describes the formation of self as taking place without the benefit of history or culture or social systems. But independence does not obliterate man's desire or need for loving relationships, and much of Whitman's poetry is more a plea for love than a defense of self-sufficiency. He advises men to trust only themselves, but also to love mankind. "All men ever born are also my brothers, and the women my sisters and lovers," he wrote. In Whitman, sex also becomes a way of relating to other human beings, but with no hint of the involvement and obligation which it often brings.

INDIVIDUALISM IN THE TWENTIETH CENTURY

The twentieth century has seen an intensification of the problem of reconciling independence and mutuality in relationships. At least as much as previously, children are trained to think and act for themselves in order to exercise good judgment in making choices. Dependency in relationships remains a great bugaboo. When the influential American behaviorist, John B. Watson, published *Psychological Care of Infant and Child* in 1928, he warned against mothers who coddled their children by kissing and fondling them. Such affection and attention were said to make the children "dependent" and to limit their capacities in "conquering the world." At the end of his book, Watson wrote that a child who can cope with the demands of American society will be "as free as possible of sensitivities to people and one who, almost from birth, is relatively independent of the family situation." Watson also recommended "boundless absorption in activity."

The consequences of Watson's advice were revealed in prose and poetry and increasingly on the psychoanalyst's couch. The frantic, frenetic searching for relationships outside the family somehow did not lead to a deep, gratifying sense of belonging. In Edgar Lee Masters' *Spoon River Anthology*—even in that small town—wife, husband, parent, and child cry out from the grave of how lonely and separate they felt, especially in relation to their closest relatives.

Poets could speak for Americans but rarely could a public man admit his private loneliness. Woodrow Wilson once did, acknowledging, "Sometimes I am a bit ashamed of myself when I think how few friends I have amidst the host of acquaintances. . . . Perhaps it is because when I give at all I want to give my whole heart, and I feel that so few want it all, or would return measure for measure. And can one as deeply covetous of friendship as I am afford to act upon such a feeling?" Here was Wilson, stern and silent, but underneath longing to give of himself, as loving and passionate as Whitman, but afraid. He probably was typical of many Americans—particularly those in the middle and upper classes and Protestant—who were afraid to act on their feelings of love because of fear of rejection and of entanglement.

The poet shows his love in fantasies on paper; the politician in abstractions in speeches and programs to save the world. Neither is as threatening as love in the closest, familial relationships with their myriad of responsibilities and obligations. Cut off from each other, countless numbers of Americans yearn to know the emotions and thoughts of another even while withholding their own. The human condition, as seen in the poetry of Robert Frost, is that man is unalterably alone. Family rarely appears. The solitude of the marital relationships described repeatedly in the literature of the twentieth century was never more poignantly spoken than in the words of the wife in "The Game of Chess" portion of T. S. Eliot's *The Wasteland*:[3]

> "My nerves are bad tonight. Yes, bad. Stay with me.
> Speak to me. Why do you never speak. Speak.
>   What are you thinking of? What thinking? What?
> I never know what you are thinking."

Whitman's urgings to love mankind outside the context of everyday relationships has been followed by many in the twentieth century. Romantic love probably remains a major way for individuals to express their need for mutuality at the same time that they declare their independence from parental authority. Romantic love now begins at an early age, sometimes in grade school, where boys and girls of nine and ten ask each other to go steady. But, to judge by the apparent increase of extramarital affairs, the clutching fervent hope for someone who will understand and allow understanding, early episodes of romantic love hardly provide a lasting sense of belonging.

Another way to love outside the context of everyday relationships is to love the family of man—as Whitman did in poetry—by giving oneself to some exhilarating cause. The world of the civil rights movement or peace movement becomes one's family circle. In my view, nothing is more important to the United States than justice for American Negroes. But people may join picket lines and sit-ins for personal reasons. In a 1965 CBS movie about unrest on the Berkeley, University of California campus, one student observed that while a picket line used to be a lonely place

[3] *Published by Harcourt, Brace & World, Inc. Used by permission of the publishers.*

(he thought) it wasn't so lonely anymore. Actually, much of the restlessness and soul-searching that now take place on college campuses grow out of profound sense of loneliness. Students often say they are reaching out for experience; but it seems to me that they are hungering for relationships. One can see it in the marijuana parties, the LSD cult, and the Tom Jones parties among the less sophisticated.

In the film about the Berkeley students, the theme is aloneness. One of the students actually says that it's difficult for young people to make changes because "we are so alone." (Ironically, it is in the traditional societies where people are not alone that changes are harder to make.) The new students are more alone than those of the 1930's because they have rejected ideology. Belonging to the Communist movement seems absurd to most of them. Society stinks, and there are no social or ideological solutions. The individual is all. As they often put it, "We're a happening, that's all." But underneath the words which speak the cult of the individual comes a crying message: "I want to be considered worthwhile"; "I want to be cared for"; "I want to believe in something." The plea to "make love, not war" is much more than a call for sexual license. It is a cry for caring.

When the Berkeley students and others at large universities say they want the university to treat them as individuals, an older generation (including professors) who also went to large and impersonal universities, and who had to work to support their families at the same time, and who were not assisted by adjustment and guidance counselors, shake their heads in bewilderment because they take the words of the students literally. It seems to me that the students are complaining not about a mass university but about a mass society based on the cult of the individual. It is the mass society which is the most individualistic, as de Tocqueville saw. The students look at the torn, broken and unhappy marriages of their parents' generation. They understand the hypocrisy which lies behind the easy pieties and moralisms of their elders. There was never more opportunity for the expression of individual talents or beliefs, but, imbued with the cult of individualism even while suffering from it, they feel squelched, suffocated, and unheard. The culture has put them on their own; they suffer from it; and they ask for more. The words come out: "We want to live our own lives . . . leave us alone." The feeling comes out: "We want to love and be loved; we want to care and be cared for."

THE PSYCHOTHERAPY OF AND FOR INDIVIDUALISM

Many of them and their parents express the same words and feeling to psychotherapists (many of whom go into that and other helping professions such as social work because of their own sense of aloneness). Psychotherapists in and out of hospitals or prisons increasingly hear such expressions as: "No one cares about me; and I don't care about anyone else"; "It's every man for himself"; "Life is just a rat race"; "Life is a snake pit"; or, "I feel so terribly alone." Often patients are so isolated and afraid that they are not able to express strong emotional feelings at all. A caring psychotherapist, whatever his training or orientation or techniques, can at least provide a relationship which may make the difference between discomfort and despair. Whatever the approach—psychoanalysis, client-centered therapy, situation therapy, art therapy, direct analysis, and so on—a warm, sensitive psychotherapist can give patients a sense of being cared for and of being permitted to express one's feelings without danger.

Much of psychotherapy seeks to heal the wounds of separateness caused by the cultural injunction of independence by helping the patient or client to become more self-sufficient. Thus the culture defines both the source of the problem and its cure. In a sense, self-sufficiency or independence psychotherapy is a prescription to adjust or conform to the culture's dominant theme. The therapist asks, as would Emerson, How can I help my client to become more separate? Therapy often results in a clearer definition and acceptance of self on the part of the patient and not infrequently with a rejection of spouse, parent, siblings, or others who are seen as interfering, controlling influences. Often, no doubt, the patient feels better for having "freed himself." But while the problem of separation has, at least for a while, been resolved, the question of belonging remains.

The most influential psychiatrists and psychologists in America have revealed an enormous preoccupation with the problem of personal independence in the assertion of self. William James consistently repeated psychological principles found in Emerson, who had been his father's good friend. Harry Stack Sullivan widely influenced American psychiatry with an emphasis on interpersonal relationships appropriate to a culture where relationships are not prescriptive but elective and therefore uncertain. Gardner Murphy had no doubt that "whatever the self is, it becomes a center . . . a supreme value." Carl Rogers, perhaps the most influential American psychotherapist, has consistently, although usually implicitly, made personal independence the supreme test of emotional maturity (acceptance and caring stem from genuine separateness).

American psychiatrists and psychologists have not emphasized the relationship of pathology to the ideology of self-sufficiency as have some of the most influential European psychiatrists such as Karen Horney, Erich Fromm, and Andras Angyal, who were raised in Europe but whose professional work developed in the United States. Horney, in her book *The Neurotic Personality of Our Time*, particularly pioneered in explaining how the cultural values of independence and achievement help to promote neuroses. Horney, Fromm, and Angyal have all stressed that low self-esteem or an underlying feeling of worthlessness is characteristic of the sick personality, and that low self-esteem can result from the extraordinary demands on self

which are made by American culture. Increasingly, psychotherapists are realizing that it is not enough to belong only
to the human race and they are asking of their patients, "To
what do you belong? To whom, and what does it mean?"

COMBINING INDEPENDENCE AND CARING

One way of reconciling the cult of independence (or some
may prefer to call it the need to be separate) with the
need for belonging is through some form of group therapy
session. Small groups, whether they are called therapy
groups, basic encounter groups, process groups, workshops,
or whatever—especially when they are made up of persons
who do not have to deal with each other in everyday life—
have enormous appeal; and it takes no unusual prescience
to predict that they will sweep the country and perhaps be
as popular as the religious revivals of the 1730's and 1830's,
which also helped to overcome loneliness.

Small group training laboratories have been used for
many years in industry, particularly under the leadership
of the National Training Laboratories at Bethel, Maine, in
order to facilitate more open and effective communication
among business executives. In recent years they have been
used in a variety of contexts, particularly on the West Coast.
Where the group members are strangers, it gives them an
extraordinary opportunity to get and give love without the
continuing responsibility and obligations of a family relationship. Not much is known about the process except
through impressions. Its proponents hope that in the unde-
manding, accepting atmosphere of the group, self-aware-
ness and the ability to communicate are enhanced; and
there is ample testimony of such an outcome from many
who have participated in such groups. Feelings of caring,
warmth, and sexuality are released which seemed stuck or
repressed before. The great fear that Woodrow Wilson had
that he could not afford to let his feelings go is diminished
in the safety of a group whose other members appear to

have the same feelings. These feelings are allowed to come into an expanded more sensitive awareness, and awareness is communicated in words and actions in a context of caring. It is possible that the group process at its best will be more than a palliative for the affliction of loneliness, and, because it is often powerful, have a transforming effect which makes itself felt in continuing relationships outside the group.

This brief description of small groups as they relate to the problems of separateness and belonging does not indicate the wide variety of groups which are now meeting. They include prayer groups, groups in businesses and educational institutions, couples groups and family groups. But the main point of them all is to help people to become more effective in their relationships with others. The point of the effectiveness may be different and the quality and character of the relationships in the group may vary greatly. The appeal may also be strictly utilitarian or achievement-centered, such as getting higher profits, a smoother administration, and so on, but the basic underlying appeal which will make groups of strangers (they don't stay strangers for long) popular is that they provide an opportunity for deep relationships without having to pay the price of continuing responsibilities and "controlling" influences.

Other more specialized groups have found semipermanent substitutes for the family to provide a sense of belonging. One of the most famous is Synanon, which began on the West Coast but is now spreading, and consists of groups of drug addicts who come together within an institutional framework with a hierarchy of authority not unlike that of an old-fashioned family. Through basic encounters in groups, individuals are encouraged to be aware of their feelings and communicate them directly. Living together under one roof causes conflicts to develop, and negative as well as positive feelings are communicated. Honesty as well as caring in relationships is vital to the process. In fact, honesty is one test of caring. Like extended families in traditional societies, Synanon provides a structure of support and discipline in which members develop a sense of obligation toward and responsibility for each other.

A comparable organization called Self-Development Group (SDG) has started in Massachusetts at the West Concord State Reformatory for Men. Prisoners participate in small basic encounter groups of ten, where they discard facades and defenses in order to achieve direct, honest, and caring communication with each other. The power of Synanon and SDG has already been demonstrated by remarkably low rates of return to drugs or crime. The controls of these new families are obviously powerful. Fierce loyalty to the group develops and it is extremely important not to let the group down. Seemingly, shame has replaced guilt as the vital check on individual deviance as it has been for centuries in the traditional family or other group-centered cultures. The sense of belonging is strong. Dependence on drugs or crime has been given up, but not for independence. A new type of family with family controls and demanding dependency relationships has been created to make up for the failures—if my assumptions are right— of the dispersive, atomistic families from which most of the members of Synanon and SDG have come.

The vast majority of Americans are neither drug addicts nor criminals; but they remain lonely. During the last twenty years, mothers have come a long way from the Watsonian formulas for promoting self-sufficiency. Watson has been replaced as a guide to child care by Benjamin Spock, whose *Baby and Child Care*, first published in 1949, has become an all-time best seller. Spock wants mothers to be flexible and comfortable in relationships with their children, but he cannot avoid the imperatives of the culture, and reminds mothers that children should not be tied to their apron strings. They need to "wean themselves from their dependence." They need an opportunity to do things on their own, "to think up projects and work them out."

Spock-reared children probably no less than those raised under the guidance of Watson are looked to for individual independence and achievement. American children in the 1960's are certainly no less famous for their self-centeredness, activity, and precocity than they were in previous times.

Cross-cultural comparisons of children—whether in films, or in literature, psychoanalysis, or behavioral studies —reveal that the American ideal is still the self-sufficient child who insists on his rights. If we are to judge by popular television programs and games, children are more in a hurry to be on their own than ever before, and middle-class parents push them as hard as they ever did. A major difference between the middle of the twentieth century and the previous eras is that there are fewer chores to do for middle-class children, fewer opportunities for a sense of of achievement. At the same time that affluence makes achievement and a sense of independence through work less accessible, it makes achievement and independence through imitation of adult play and social relations, not only more accessible but more necessary to fill the void. The middle-class mother rushes her child into nursery school just as quickly as possible so that he will learn to be on his own and develop proper motor and social skills. The nursery school—like the television set—becomes more important not only because the child must learn to be free from mother, but because mom has to be free from the tensions of her relationship with junior or to fulfill or actualize herself in achievements of her own apart from her roles as wife and mother. Let the child turn all that energy onto his playmates or teacher or into identification with "Secret Agent" or "The Man from U.N.C.L.E." Middle-class parents who dread the summer vacation when classes and the best television programs are suspended can send their children to summer camp and thrill to every achievement from passing the deep-end test to learning how to dance with members of the opposite sex at age nine.

NEW EXPRESSIONS OF THE CULT OF INDEPENDENCE

It would be surprising if children who came out of highly dispersive, competitive families in which each member strove for self-assertion to reach some kind of self-fulfillment did not reach adolescence with both a strong sense of resentment against ties which bind and a terrible feeling of loneliness and need to belong. The results in the 1960's can be seen in the dances and songs of the young and in the cult of "cool." The frug, the watusi, and the what-have-you may mean many things, but they appear to signify at least in part a frenetic attempt at self-expression, a crying to be heard. The most popular teen-age songs of the 1960's unquestionably reveal a frenzied concern about parents who stifle one's independence alongside of an urgent plea for caring relationships. But there is a danger in relationships which bind, if we are to believe the language of the cool world. Maintaining one's cool means not getting committed or overly involved. The ideal is not to be tied down; it is to keep swinging, spinning in orbit, or even to take a trip way, way out.

At a deeper philosophical level, many college students and intellectuals have found a philosophical justification for the cult of independence in existentialism. In the existential thought of Kierkegaard, Sartre, and others, "subjectivity is the starting point." Man is responsible to and for himself alone. There are no oughts (except that one). "Action precedes essence," and commitments of any kind, even in relationships, are elective, not prescriptive. Existentialism has an enormous appeal in societies where traditions are being shattered, values overturned, and men split off from each other. In the United States it has special appeal because it supports the preeminent value of personal independence. But it does not answer, any more than did Emerson or Whitman, man's constant cry for belonging.

Because the value of personal independence promotes

elective rather than prescriptive relationships, it means that relations in the United States have tended to be contractual. Commitments, not being prescriptive, depend upon continuity in the circumstances which led to the contract. They are very much like that old principle of Roman law, *rebus sic stantibus* (things being what they are), which vitiates the validity of international agreements if circumstances change. Things are never what they were, which is why international law and contractual human relationships are so tenuous—and apprehension and anxiety concerning relationships become the rule. That is why youngsters often advise each other to maintain their cool and avoid getting hurt by being overcommitted. Contractual relationships, as Erich Fromm pointed out, abide by the market principle. In his view, many Americans are equipped with a mental calculus which helps them determine how much there is in it for them in any given relationship.

The volunteer movement in the United States, in which the Peace Corps plays a major role, provides a significant new opportunity for personal independence and achievement, but it also opens up the possibility of meaningful relationships. Those who have participated in the tutoring of educationally disadvantaged children, or worked with Indians on reservations, or have helped migrant laborers with their myriad of problems, and have opened themselves up in relationship to those they serve agree with Peace Corps volunteers that they learn more than they teach. The major difference between Peace Corps volunteers and the others is that the Peace Corpsmen serve in another culture in which relationships are usually defined by traditional kinship, tribal, or village patterns. The mutuality they experience—what the boy from South Carolina called mutualness—is bound up in a network of interdependent relationships. The people they learn to enjoy are not governed by the values of personal independence and achievement but by some version of *utang na loob, paki-kisama,* and *bahala na.*

:

What follows is even more speculative than what has gone before. The speculations advanced above and those below flow primarily from my study of American history, the sociology of ethnic groups in the United States, the experience of Americans overseas, my limited knowledge of psychological pathology and psychotherapy in the United States and other countries, and also from my personal experience as Director of the Peace Corps in the Philippines, and from my work with the Self-Development Group in Massachusetts.

The underlying assumption of much of what I have written in this chapter is that the cult of self-sufficiency is a cause of or at least is related to a widespread sense of loneliness, meaninglessness, and worthlessness in American life. There is little of what scientists could call proof to support this hypothesis, although there is a considerable amount of systematic evidence. I have written without making sharp distinctions between neuroses, psychoses, and a general malaise of atomism which I relate hypothetically to Adamism. Transcultural studies are new, and cross-cultural studies in psychological pathology and health are only just beginning. Even if we knew that there were more autistic children in the United States than China, and even if we knew that the disease of autism was related to cultural values and social systems (which we do not), it still might be impossible to demonstrate that widespread autism of children in the United States resulted from the cult of individualism.

HOW VOLUNTEERS ARE CHANGED

It seems to me that one of the most important ways in which Peace Corps volunteers in the Philippines have been changed is that they have become not only more sensitive and caring in their own relationships, but that they have become much more aware of the loneliness and emptiness of many human relationships in the United States. A boy from South Carolina who spent two extra years in the Philippines wrote after returning home: "As I mentioned in my last letter, alienation is the big thing here. . . . People are so alone, so lonely, so desiring to give themselves and yet holding themselves back at the same time . . . the urge to be separate, to not touch the other or open to the other, is very strong." He had experienced the loving warmth of close familial relationships in the Philippines and was made acutely aware of the impersonal and competitive character of American life.

Warmth, closeness, lovingness, and dependability often appear to characterize the relationships in families of traditional cultures. This is not to say that depth in relationships is characteristic of those cultures. (Nor is it to say that other cultures are free from their own kinds of neuroses and psychoses.) Anthropologists in the South Seas have often noticed what appears to them to be an unwillingness to become deeply involved with others. But there is a quality of give and take, ebb and flow, and mutuality which volunteers experienced in the Philippines and elsewhere which seemed to many of them and to me to be strikingly lacking among Americans.

To learn this by living it is vastly different from learning it by reading about it, even if one accepts the evidence presented here. The volunteers, at least many of them, took the time to care. Living in a Filipino village for two years without any possibility of a raise or promotion, without any need to manipulate others, they could afford to show their caring. One boy wrote that Filipinos will remember "the little things that showed I cared for them, drinking *tuba* and dancing folk dances and singing folk songs, talking to them in their own language, the thousand and one things that go into meaningful relationships whether a word or not has ever been spoken." Dozens of other volunteers concluded that their capacity to give and receive love in relationships had been developed through their exposure to Filipinos in the villages. In this, the Peace Corps volunteers of the Philippines are not alone. Although Peace Corps programs and the attitudes of the Peace Corps Directors vary considerably from country to country, volunteers from every continent have told of becoming more sensitive and caring in their relationships. They have also reacted to harsh impersonality in the United States.

The change in volunteers is a corollary of their awareness of a certain kind of underdevelopment in the United States. It is an understanding that Americans have been so busy getting and doing that their capacity for being in relationships with others, particularly those closest to them in their own families, has been blunted. In the Philippines, the emphasis on smooth interpersonal relationships did not make volunteers value honesty less, but it made them appreciate sensitivity and caring more. In some respects, volunteers become more capable of thinking and judging for themselves, and in that sense more self-reliant than before, but having known the joys of *pakikisama,* which is so closely related to *utang na loob,* they now also know, if they did not before, the relationship between self-reliance and loneliness.

A NEW CONCEPT OF DEVELOPMENT

The experience of Peace Corps volunteers indicates the need for a completely revised concept of development. Productivity is undoubtedly one aspect of human development, but it is far from the only measure, and it seems to me that Americans—having emphasized productivity so much—have been severely handicapped in developing other aspects of their humanness. Autonomy or self-direction, if defined in terms of the capacity of individuals to have a self-integrated understanding of their experience and to communicate that experience, is also, it seems to me, an aspect of human development. But a people which has emphasized self-sufficiency to the extent that has been true in the United States have in this way also limited certain aspects of their humanness.

The Peace Corps is primarily an instrument of human development, not just economic development. Filipinos and others unquestionably change in the direction of Western, and particularly American, values as a result of contact with volunteers, although the changes may be much slower than many people had thought they would be. But Americans change too. As one girl from Wisconsin said of her Filipina teacher friend, "I affected her life, because she affected mine . . . we wanted to experience each other." They affected each other because their experiencing of each other went beyond the ordinary qualities of friendship between persons from the same culture. By being involved in each other they were involved in each other's cultures. It is possible to read about other cultures but it is highly unlikely that one can become involved in them through reading. Being involved, as one ex-Peace Corps volunteer put it, has "the power of giving pain or pleasure." This boy, who had served in Nigeria, understood as profoundly as any Peace Corps volunteer from the Philippines that it was the emotional experiencing of the other culture through relationships with individuals which changed him. He has written: "This to me is the meaning of the Peace Corps . . . it is the call to go, not where man has never been before, but where he has lived differently; the call to experience firsthand the intricacies of a different culture; to understand from the inside rather than the outside; and to test the limits of one's own way of life against another." [4]

It seems to me that from watching the encounter of Peace Corps volunteers in relationship to Filipinos that the American cult of individualism has severely limited the human development of Americans in certain aspects even

[4] *This is from a superb short pamphlet by David Shickele, called "When the Right Hand Washes the Left,"* A Peace Corps Discussion Paper, 1966.

while advancing it in others. It also appears to me that where encounter between Filipinos and Americans was penetrating and sustained, changes took place on both sides leading, in Teilhard de Chardin's conception, toward the convergence and complexification of man. By convergence, de Chardin meant the tendency of men to incorporate the results of differentiation into an organized unified pattern. Man is the only successful species that has remained as a single interbreeding group or species; rather than diffusing biologically as do birds or other species, he converges through biological fusion and cultural diffusion toward a union of the whole human species. But while the family of man emerges, individuals become more complex and differentiated.

Filipinos and American Peace Corps volunteers became more alike in some ways, even as they became more aware of their differences, each side tending to draw from the culture of the other those aspects of man's humanness which seemed lacking in themselves and yet attractive. The process of change of fundamental values and personality characteristics within great cultures is slow, but it is going on all the time and will now be speeded by the increasing number of human encounters that take place across cultures. Human behavior is a sum of beliefs, values, attitudes, feelings, words, and other actions which constantly interact and affect each other. It seems impossible to me to say that feelings are always prior to beliefs or values, or vice versa. One feels something about women, nature, or God and what one feels is in part determined by beliefs which have been handed down for generations of men whose feelings in relationship to women, nature, or God helped shape those beliefs. One speaks or acts out of beliefs or values or attitudes or feelings, or a combination of them, but action itself affects beliefs, values, attitudes, and feelings.

All human societies are underdeveloped, and there are probably no men in any culture who have not suffered from spiritual, emotional, physical, or aesthetic underdevelopment. Many Filipinos (and undoubtedly other Asians too) even when they are critical of excessive individualism and activity in Americans, begin, after long contact with them, to value the individual freedom of Americans not only to make choices for themselves but to communicate more openly and directly with persons in authority. While they may recognize that excessive individualism can lead to loneliness and selfishness, they also feel the extent to which the emphasis in their own culture on family-centered group cohesion has inhibited certain aspects of their personal development. Americans, after becoming involved in individuals from the more traditional cultures, if they follow the experience of many Peace Corps volunteers, will feel that aspects of their own development have been hindered by the highly individualistic, planful, and purposeful culture in which they have been reared. They may like political democracy and economic prosperity no less than before but see something more. For surely Americans are far behind others in their capacity to appreciate and understand mystery, or in expressing their bodies freely and rhythmically, or in absorbing and merging confidently and harmoniously with nature, or in feeling the joys of mutuality in relationships. In these ways, Peace Corps volunteers and other Americans will be changed through deep and lasting personal encounter with other cultures even as Africans, Latin Americans, Asians, Polynesians, and others are changed by Americans toward more rational, scientific ways of perception and cognition and toward more independent and achievement-centered behavior. Cultures will converge but individuals will become more complex. We are entering the age of multicultural personalities whose identities, being complex, are uncertain and who suffer pain because of that uncertainty. We inherit in our cradles our cultural values and our styles of thinking and acting, but they are subject to change as a result of personal encounter with others holding different values.

Studies show that thus far modifications of personality

as a result of intercultural experience are infrequent, but that is because the experiences are rarely as penetrating or sustained as they were for many Peace Corps volunteers in the Philippines. If we are to judge by the experience of some of them, Americans may develop their abilities to give and receive love as a result of basic personal encounter with Asians, even if it means becoming involved in relationships which prescribe continuity of commitment and obligation. Americans may become less self-reliant as they feel the beauty of belonging in relationships, even when it means counting on others and being depended on by them. They may learn to reject Emerson's advice to "unhand me" and even see certain consequences of the cult of self-sufficiency as barbaric and unhuman. Whether this will be done in families or in other new, perhaps experimental, relationships, or both, seems to me more risky to predict than that it will be done.

It is already being done by those who join basic encounter or therapy groups in search of more caring relationships. But this does not mean that the ideology of independence has been abandoned. For many, the central issue is no longer independence versus dependence but independence for what?

If I understand many young Americans correctly, they are saying they no longer want independence geared toward either production or consumption. They no longer want to be either inner-directed (in the driven, Puritan sense) or other-directed (in the market-oriented sense) men and women. They value productivity less than their grandfathers and consumption less than their fathers, but they cling steadfastly to the ideology of independence. Now they speak of independence to fulfill or actualize themselves, but that often is seen as coming—at least in part—through intimate, caring relationships. It seems as if a growing number of Americans want what they call self-direction or autonomy plus a greater sense of belonging. In the past a sense of belonging has implied more than caring for and being cared about and even more than sharing with others. As Peace Corps volunteers from the Philippines know, it has meant being counted on by others, being responsible for others, and being obligated to others. It is these three concepts—being counted on, responsible for, and obligated to *others*—that cause many Americans discomfort. They hope to get the caring and sharing aspects of belonging through an interpersonal commitment which grows out of the existential situation without being tied down or made dependent. It is an ambitious and possibly illusory goal.

Those who hold this point of view maintain that self-direction or autonomy does not preclude belonging relationships as long as they are elective and not prescriptive. It is all right to belong as long as one is free not to belong. In fact, some advocates of this view see autonomy as the basis of a loving relationship which is deeper because it is more free. Psychologist Abraham Maslow makes the distinction between "insecure" and "secure autonomy." Insecure autonomy is the strength of personality as over and against the world, causing the person to see himself and others as being mutually exclusive. Secure autonomy, according to Maslow, means that one has affection for the world and others and that there is a feeling of trust in and identity with others. But in the past, having affection for and identity with others usually has meant being tied to them, and not in an elective, contractual way. I think most people who have experienced the emotion of love in a belonging relationship would say it has to do with giving oneself to another to enhance the other over a period of time, including feelings of being counted on by, responsible for, and obligated to, them.

Whether Americans become more or less autonomous seems to me to be almost irrelevant. They will become more human. To borrow a conception from philosopher Martin Buber, they will be less individuals and more persons. Individuals emphasize their separateness from others. Persons engage in a dynamic I-Thou relationship which is an encounter of interfering as well as accepting love. Individuals are preoccupied with protecting their separate selves apart from others. Persons are concerned with expressing themselves in society and relationship to others. Are individuals or persons more autonomous? If words mean anything at all, there is no such thing as the autonomous human being. We are the creatures of our cultures, as the American celebration of autonomy and self-sufficiency shows. Development, if we are to judge from the experience of Peace Corps volunteers and Filipinos, cannot be measured on an autonomy or a dependency scale. It is something which transcends culturally biased oversimplifications.

The nature of human change in the process of human development remains largely a mystery, but surely it is something more grand and complex than what Americans have seen as direction toward self-sufficiency. That is undeniably a part of our development as humans, but only a part. To care and be cared for, to have a sense of belonging, also has to do with our development as human beings. As one Peace Corps volunteer in the Philippines wrote, his relationships with Filipinos "gave me ties . . . and gave me sudden inexplicable intimations of brotherhood with all people." The emerging family of man will not be Americanized, Europeanized, Africanized, or shaped only by Asian values. It will be, if the Peace Corps gives us a clue, a family that increasingly appreciates the marvels of mystery as well as the symmetry of science, the peace of passivity as well as the power of productivity, and the balm of belonging as well as the satisfaction of self-sufficiency.

A personal afterword

: In reading the manuscript of this book before sending it to the publisher, I was struck by how much I had left out concerning my personal experience in the Peace Corps. Even now, I recall the first eight months of Peace Corps administration in the Philippines with astonishment. The tasks we took upon ourselves required constant attention and exhausting inputs of energy: finding houses for three hundred volunteers, a Peace Corps office in Manila, and four field offices; contacting principals and teachers at several hundred schools; explaining the Peace Corps to Filipino officials and the press; studying and discussing requests from more than thirty Filipino agencies desiring new programs; organizing medical care for volunteers; establishing in-country training programs; preparing dialect training materials and institutes; greeting, entertaining, and guiding approximately forty visitors from Washington; attempting to strengthen a vaguely and weakly conceived program; and— most enervating of all—dealing with daily crises in the health and morale of volunteers.

One of the earliest disheartening occurrences was the decision of the first volunteer from Group 1 to resign from the Peace Corps. An idealist and capable teacher who was respected and admired by staff and volunteers, she made up her mind that she could do more for her country and herself by returning to the United States to teach. Nothing I could say dissuaded her, although we argued past 2 A.M. I felt badly defeated.

Later, when the programs in the Philippines and the Peace Corps around the world were firmly established, I did not attempt to argue with volunteers who were determined to leave; but at that time, when the Peace Corps in the field was yet unproved, and when approximately one third of all Peace Corps volunteers in the world were in the Philippines, I feared that her example might set off a stampede of resignations.

One of the reasons we worked unusually hard in the early months was that Peace Corps overseas administration was designed to be understaffed. It was generally accepted as gospel at Peace Corps headquarters that volunteers would be able to take care of themselves. A Peace Corps Representative (he was not called a Director at first) would be needed to represent the new agency to Filipinos and Americans, conduct negotiations on new programs, and to handle emergencies; but it was thought that there would be no need for a staff to give administrative or logistic support (that would be done by AID) or to provide supervisory support on the job (that would be done by the host country agency to which volunteers were assigned) or to give training (that was the responsibility of universities in the United States).

Each of these assumptions was wrong; but they were

held with such tenacity in the early days that the staffing plan for the first year in the Philippines called for a Representative, a deputy, one additional staff member, and a medical doctor. Although I was as naïve as many others in underestimating the magnitude of overseas administrative responsibilities, I did succeed in obtaining an agreement to increase the size of my staff by two additional field representatives. Now I am astonished to recall that we thought six men (including myself and a medical doctor) could give anything close to adequate support to three hundred volunteers who would be asked to perform a vague job spread over large distances in a strange environment.

My earliest reactions to fatigue, disappointment, and problems in the Philippines were characteristic of my personality (at least at that point). No matter how rough things became for volunteers or staff in training or in the field, my public face was constantly enthusiastic. I talked about wonderful Filipinos, magnificent opportunities for service and personal growth, and of the happy prospects for future success for the Peace Corps in the Philippines. I believed what I said, but at a subconscious level I must have felt far less certain about the prospects of the program. It was not until five months had passed that I was comfortable and objective enough to give appropriate empathy to the pain, frustration, and hostility of volunteers.

I was not so foolish that I failed to see within a few weeks that we were seriously understaffed. Six weeks after the first volunteers arrived I wrote a memorandum to Washington urging the appointment of at least one more field representative. I also had the temerity to suggest that technical personnel be added to my staff, including two training officers who were experts in community development and education. The memorandum resulted in my being recalled to Washington where I won agreement to adding one more man to my staff.

It had become clear that the four basic assumptions underlying the Peace Corps policy of understaffing simply did not hold up—at least not in the Philippines. The volunteers were not supermen and -women who could take care of themselves. A large proportion of them ignored basic health rules, and a larger number were in need of counseling and leadership.

AID did not provide overall effective administrative support. Rather, AID officials—with some exceptions—frequently hampered me and my staff in attempting to cut red tape to get supplies, process vouchers, and otherwise provide logistic support to volunteers in the field.

The Philippines Bureau of Public Schools did not provide supervisory support on the job. Only one official in Manila had been assigned as liaison with the Peace Corps (he was a generalist like me with no special competence in teaching English or science), and provincial officials were usually prevented by cultural inhibitions from taking responsibility for supervision.

The university training program in the United States provided none of the following: language instruction (although some excellent lectures were given on general linguistics); an opportunity for practice teaching; instruction in using the English language manuals being developed in the Philippines; simulation training through direct exposure to another culture or subculture; or sensitivity training through participation in basic encounter or sensitivity groups.[1]

In addition, one medical doctor was hopelessly inadequate for the task of organizing and administering medical care for three hundred volunteers.

There were five long-range solutions for these problems, all of which were accomplished either shortly before or immediately after I left the Philippines. Completed before my departure were:

[1] *Considering the fact that no one had ever run a training program for Peace Corps volunteers before, it would have been a minor miracle if the university had not made whopping mistakes. Its program was no more didactic and sedentary than most Peace Corps training programs; and its conscientious staff was more aware than I or my staff of the cultural resistance which Peace Corps volunteers would meet in attempting to do their jobs.*

1. Much greater involvement on the part of the Bureau of Public Schools in supporting the work of the volunteers.
2. The appointment to my staff of a specialist in science education (a precedent which later made possible the appointment of other specialists).
3. The selection of new universities in the United States for more effective training, including language instruction.

After my departure, my successor as Peace Corps Director in the Philippines accomplished the following:

1. Control over administrative and logistics support by the elimination of AID as the administrative support agency for the Peace Corps.
2. Doubling the size of his staff, including the appointment of a deputy director for management and another deputy director for programming (I had had no deputy).
3. An increase in the number of medical doctors from one to four.

These steps were taken—and rightly so—even though the number of volunteers in the Philippines went down from six hundred to four hundred.

Before these long range solutions could be achieved, two important actions were taken. One was to make the fullest use of a category of volunteers, called volunteer leaders, provided by the Peace Corps Act. In effect, they were given staff responsibilities, and they frequently attended staff meetings and participated in making major decisions.

Another short term action in dealing with the problem of staff shortage was the utilization of Filipino personnel in positions of high responsibility. I appointed one Filipino-American psychiatrist, who had held important positions in community development and health programs in the Philippines, to help in counseling volunteers. I found an extremely able Filipino employee of AID to take the responsibility for coordinating Peace Corps administrative work. The third person, a Filipina, was chosen to take responsibility for office affairs. These three Filipinos (the first was actually a United States citizen) participated in key staff decisions and actions at the highest level, often to the astonishment and dismay of Americans in other agencies.

Despite these steps, everyone on my staff had to work without regard for health or personal or family pleasure for the first eight months, when there were few nights of normal sleep or weekends that were not given to working.

Staff reactions to the almost daily personnel crises and other fatiguing problems varied. One staff member fell back under pressure and left the Philippines by mutual consent after the first year. Another, who had brilliantly diagnosed some of the critical problems of the program, left because of his disagreements with Washington. A third seemed to me to me unhappy much of the time. A fourth, the medical doctor, found it difficult to bear up under the impossible task of organizing medical care for three hundred volunteers in more than one hundred locations spread throughout the archipelago; he also left by mutual consent after one year.

Of the original staff, only one held up day after day under the most incredible pressure. First he organized the program for approximately seventy-five volunteers in the Bicol region where he lived with his family; later he took charge of the entire program for 275 volunteers in Mindanao, where he lived also with his family in a simple, nipa-style house. But even this iron man—it seemed he never took time away from his job—would fall into bed for ten to twelve hours after an extended trip to the hinterlands.

My concession to pressure was to develop walking bronchitis (the most common disease in the Philippines) and (after several days of skipped lunches and unusual pressure) a duodenal ulcer.

I certainly was delighted to see three new staff men and a doctor as replacements for the three men who had departed at the end of the first year. Apparently I had picked up an extra man in exchange, which was important since six hundred volunteers would soon be on duty in the Philippines; but one of the new men, alleged to be proficient in management, had to be fired because of inefficiency. However, one of the new field men (still with the Peace Corps in Washington) turned out to be another iron man, thank goodness, and the new medical doctor brought considerable administrative strength to his area of concern.

Of all the problems I faced none was more enervating than the inefficient and dishonest behavior of one key man in Washington. This man—no longer with the Peace Corps —seemed to me to be typical of a few others in the agency who appeared much more concerned with making a success for themselves than for the Peace Corps. But the danger presented by his behavior was not due to personal ambition. All of the top men in the Peace Corps were highly ambitious and Sargent Shriver welcomed their personal drive. Because this man was incompetent, important requests to him for information went unanswered, pleas for additional staff were ignored, and information meant for training institutions was not passed on. Because he was dishonest, he defended himself against criticism with evasiveness or lies. In addition, he made no serious effort to understand the basic problems of the program and was thoroughly insensitive to Filipinos. Of course, he might see himself quite differently; but this is the way that I and the members of my staff and the volunteers who had anything to do with him perceived him.

Another serious problem during my tenure as director was AID in Manila. Certain program officials in AID were extremely helpful to the Peace Corps, including Richard Bernhardt, later Deputy Director of AID in the Philippines, George Spencer, a community development expert who is now on the Peace Corps staff, and Ed Parfrey, a young program officer. Relationships with these men were excellent, but they were not charged with the task of providing

for the Peace Corps nuts and bolts, administrative and logistic support, which, to describe it most charitably, was
erratic.

AID procedures simply were not geared to a field operation like the Peace Corps. AID normally worked with a
long lead time and with fewer emergencies in getting supplies to technicians and processing their vouchers for reim-
bursement. But differences in procedures accounted for
only part of our difficulties with AID. Many persons, including Peace Corps officials and volunteers, viewed the
very birth and existence of the Peace Corps as a criticism
of AID officials for living in golden ghettos, using the PX
and chauffeured government cars, and not learning the language and culture of their hosts. One volunteer actually
made an unfair critical attack on AID to a Filipino audience in Manila, for which I rebuked him severely.

It took some time before certain executive-office officials
of AID realized that neither I nor my staff would follow
their pattern of working and living. We rebuffed suggestions to settle in American neighborhoods, send our children to the American school, be driven to and from work
or lunch in chauffeured cars, or even join the American Sea-
front Compound where families of United States personnel
can swim, relax, and eat in mainland comfort. That I drove
a jeep in Manila must have seemed bizarre to AID officials
(and I now think they were correct), but even more, it
may have seemed a reproach. I could never escape the feeling that the Peace Corps, whether we wanted it or not, was
a living reprimand to AID.

To further complicate our relationship, AID appeared
to be phasing out in the Philippines. The Peace Corps was
on the way up. AID was under constant attack by Congress
and the White House, but among the many agencies in
Washington, the Peace Corps was fairest of them all. Two
high AID officials asked me to consider them for Peace
Corps employment, and it seemed to me that my failure
to recommend them hindered the support we received

from AID. Regardless of these factors, the Peace Corps could not—at least so I was instructed—adopt its own procedures for giving administrative, logistic, and fiscal support to volunteers, and could not even control the personnel assigned by AID to give us those services. Payment for those services was charged to the Peace Corps according to an agreement worked out in Washington, where my protest of the high amount charged was ignored despite the fact that AID officials repeatedly refused to alter their procedures to meet our needs.

Not every administrative difficulty could be blamed on AID. Checks mailed by the United States Treasury in Manila were sometimes delayed in getting to volunteers in the field. Repeatedly I asked experts in AID, the Peace Corps, and the Treasury Department to come up with an alternative means of paying volunteers, but no one could think of anything within regulations that would be more satisfactory. After my tenure the problem was solved by the imaginative procedure of setting up limited checking accounts for volunteers which, in effect, provided them with money in advance of expenditures (although I understand that this system is now being abandoned because it has created other problems).

One difficulty that could be blamed on neither AID nor the Treasury but was squarely my own responsibility was the inadequate methods of fiscal accounting that we employed in the field. No action ever was taken outside of the law or regulations and we were conservative in spending the taxpayer's money, but our accounting procedures properly raised the eyebrows of auditors who did not realize that the Peace Corps was—from a fiscal point of view— more like the army in the field than AID. Sometimes staff members made purchases for volunteers with their own money rather than wait for supplies to arrive through normal channels.

While the inevitable bickering and politicking that goes on between and within agencies caused considerable personal discomfort, my greatest concern—aside from day-to-day personnel crises of volunteers—was to obtain a continuing commitment from the host-country agency, the Bureau of Public Schools, to become involved in sharpening and defining the tasks that the volunteers were to perform to give them support in carrying out those tasks. Happily, such involvement was accomplished to a considerable extent, although too late to be of much help to volunteers from the earliest groups.

Happily, too, the irritations and frustrations of my life as Peace Corps Director were eclipsed by rich pleasures that came from working with many wonderful and effective people: other American officials, particularly in the embassy; Peace Corps staff members; volunteers and volunteer leaders; and Filipino co-workers and friends.

Our relationships at the embassy were quite good. I received wonderful personal support from the two men who served as Chiefs of Mission, Gordon Mein, now Ambassador to Guatemala, and Ambassador William Stevenson, a former president of Oberlin College. Stevenson occasionally visited volunteers in the field and twice called on our national in-service training center near Zamboanga.

Three younger men on the embassy staff, Gerald Rosen, Carl McMillan, and Frank Tatu were highly intelligent, dedicated professionals who were extremely helpful to the Peace Corps in a variety of ways.

Sargent Shriver gave me and my staff considerable personal encouragement, particularly in the early days when he tried to maintain close and direct relationships with his Peace Corps Representatives. Shriver's quick mind, enthusiasm, idealism, humor, and energy were extremely important to most of us, and he and I enjoyed a warm personal relationship. I regret that I did not exploit our excellent relationship more to press certain criticisms of internal Peace Corps operations and personnel, but at the time I felt that I was much too busy trying to help volunteers to take time and energy for bureaucratic in-fighting.

There were other important staff members in the Peace Corps at Washington who understood sensitively the program in the Philippines and supported it: Nicholas Hobbs, first Peace Corps Director of Research and Selection and now Provost at Vanderbilt University; Charles Peters, currently Director of Evaluation and Research of the Peace Corps; Bill Delano, the Peace Corps's first General Counsel and now head of the International Secretariat of the Peace Corps; Joseph English, the Peace Corps's Chief Psychiatrist; and Bill Moyers, who was then Deputy Director of the agency. The encouragement of these men was important to me.

Relationships with certain members of my own staff were especially gratifying. I have never seen people work as hard under such extremely difficult circumstances as Bill Warren, Roger Flather, John Cort, Harvey Pressman, Charles Dey, Larry Howard, Jack Harkness, Mary Kinsella, and John Harville. Some were more effective than others but they were all dedicated to the welfare of the volunteers and the Peace Corps.

That is also true for the key Filipinos on our staff, Bert Pumento, Mrs. Elena Borneo, and Annie Gison, who became close friends of the staff and volunteers (Annie eventually married a volunteer). They are wonderful human beings: devoted, scrupulous, intelligent, sensitive, and effective. It was not uncommon for Pumento, who was responsible for management at the Peace Corps, to greet me at the door to my office at 6:30 or 7:00 A.M., or for Mrs. Borneo, who served as office manager as well as my personal secretary, to work through dinner well into the night. They both usually attended important staff meetings and participated in the making of policy decisions. It is hard to believe that the Peace Corps could have survived without Mr. Pumento and Mrs. Borneo. They were part of a freewheeling, flexible, decision-making system in which nationality and status barriers were often broken, and in which innovative, creative administration was encouraged.

In that system, so called volunteer leaders played a crucial role. Although the authors of the Peace Corps Act who provided for the category of volunteer leader had in mind older men and women to help a small staff give counseling support to younger volunteers, few oldsters applied to the Peace Corps. We tapped young volunteers—often against their wills—to fill the position, after they had proved themselves in the field as educational aides (the first leaders were selected before they ever had a chance to do many of the tasks assigned to volunteers).

The volunteer leaders lived in the provinces, usually close to a field staff representative. They drove their battered jeeps through every kind of weather to keep lines of contact and communication open to volunteers in remote areas. They delivered supplies, mail, and even money. But the best of them became sensitive listeners and knowledgeable advisers concerning Filipino culture generally and Filipino education specifically. They were not always appreciated by other volunteers, some of whom—whether they wanted to be leaders or not—were envious of their frequent trips to Manila and Zamboanga, participation with staff and Filipino officials in making policy, and the additional twenty-five dollars a month set aside for leaders under the Peace Corps Act.

Some volunteers resented the leaders because they thought the position to be unnecessary, at least as far as they were concerned, and viewed its occupants as dropouts from the difficult, main business of living in one barrio community for two years. But most volunteers increasingly appreciated this amazingly dedicated and talented group whose stamina and resourcefulness and quiet loyalty were a constant source of encouragement to me. These men and women, whose average age probably was no more than twenty-four or twenty-five, were given responsibilities rarely extended to young people, even in war. Their situations called for tact, restraint, courage, physical strength, ingenuity, integrity, and kindness. They rarely erred; they always tried.

I have kept in touch with most of the volunteer leaders from Groups 1 through 4, many of whom hold important positions: John Bossany is a key Peace Corps staff member in the Philippines; Lionel Castillo, a candidate for the Ph.D. degree in social work at the University of Pittsburgh, is the coordinator of a community development organization in that city; Mike Foreman, completing his work for the Ph.D. degree in Southeast Asian studies at Cornell, was coordinator of language training at a Peace Corps Philippines training program in the summer of 1966; Leonard Giesecke, now in pursuit of a Ph.D. degree in economics at the University of Texas, served for two years on the Peace Corps staff in Turkey; Gerald Mullins is presently assistant director for continuing education at Marquette University; Marjory Pfankuch, who has worked as a community development organizer in West Virginia and as educational director of an experimental preschool program for slum children in Boston, is now helping to prepare new curriculum materials on the Negro in American life for Educational Services, Inc.; Ralph Thomas is a candidate for the Ph.D. degree in history at the University of Pennsylvania; Duncan Yaggy, after teaching in an experimental program at the Cardoza High School in Washington, is presently Assistant to the Director of the Social Sciences Curriculum Project at Educational Services, Inc., and a candidate for the Ph.D. degree in American civilization at Brandeis University; Becky Johnston is currently a social worker with the Jewish Welfare Service in New York; Jerry Poznak teaches high school English in Sudbury, Massachusetts; Sandra Williams Yaggy teaches elementary school in Weston, Massachusetts; Nicholas Royal is a staff member in the University of Wisconsin's Human Development Program at Milwaukee; David Szanton, who, when he was in the Philippines, did original research on the art of the Sulu

Archipelago and has played an important role in Peace Corps training programs, is a candidate for the Ph.D. degree in anthropology at the University of Chicago; Patricia Toalson Vittetow is assistant to the Dean of Students at Brandeis University; David Ziegenhagen, following two years as a staff member in Thailand, is now in charge of the Thai desk at Peace Corps headquarters in Washington; Jonathan Epstein is responsible for language training at the Peace Corps training center in Puerto Rico; Thomas Newman, who directed the Peace Corps training program at St. John's College in the summer of 1966, is on the Peace Corps training staff in Puerto Rico; Steve Wells is a regional representative on the Peace Corps staff in the Philippines; Philip Olsen heads the Peace Corps Philippines desk in Washington; James Stewart, currently a candidate for the Ph.D. degree in anthropology at the University of Hawaii, served as assistant director of the Peace Corps training program for the Philippines in Cambridge, Massachusetts, during the summer of 1966; Richard Vittetow, who directed that program, is currently a candidate for the Ph.D. degree in sociology at Brandeis University; Philip Ginsberg is studying for an advanced degree in journalism at Columbia University; Dave Christiansen is with AID in Vietnam; John Durand was recently field director of the State Democratic Party of Wisconsin; and Jennifer Grant is married to an ILO official who works in Jamaica, where they live with their baby girl.

There were several other volunteer leaders from Groups 1 through 4 who performed outstandingly in the Philippines—Philip Nicholas, Ray Meyer, Claire Horan, Eric Peterson, Susan Thompson, Virginia Cochran, Kathy Hannon, Ron Hall, and Mary Garland—but I have not kept up with their latest activities.

When the size of the staff was expanded, the need for volunteer leaders became less acute, but volunteer leaders in Groups 5 through 9 played key roles in the Philippines, too, and most of them have gone on to responsible and interesting work in the United States.

There were many volunteers with outstanding leadership ability, who, for one reason or another—in some cases they declined—did not serve as volunteer leaders, some of whom now hold significant positions in the Peace Corps itself. Two examples are Maureen Carroll from Group 1, who holds an important job in the Division of Evaluation at Peace Corps headquarters in Washington, and Ron Herring, who directed the Peace Corps training program for the Philippines at San Jose State College, California, in the summer of 1966.

Visits to volunteers in the field buoyed me. I invariably enjoyed my field trips, which, despite missed sleep, long rides over rugged roads, and occasional bad weather, were less tiring than the endless round of cables, conferences, and meetings in Manila. In fact, I usually came back from visits to the field with renewed optimism and strength. I liked direct contact with volunteers more than any other aspect of my job. I wanted to know them as human beings, not just as volunteers, and—though I was sometimes disappointed by them—a large majority reinforced my original optimism. Volunteers often were unreasonable, mixed up, and sometimes spiteful and petty; but most of them displayed a quiet courage and ability to cope with new experiences that was heartening and stimulating to me.

To the volunteers I owe much; perhaps I owe even more to the Filipinos. They taught me to see myself, my countrymen, and the human condition in new ways. They also proved that dynamic human encounters across cultural barriers, while terribly difficult to accomplish, are possible. For all that separates Americans from Filipinos, I know now from personal experience that a basic human encounter can transcend cultural differences. As I write this, I am thinking of my Filipino friends: Bert Pumento and his fine family; Elena Borneo and her wonderful family; Mike Gaffud, then the Undersecretary of Education; and Fe Manza and Aurelio Juele of the Bureau of Public Schools. Their kindness and sensitivity kept me from being even more awkward and confused in my relationships with Filipinos than I otherwise would have been. But more importantly, we met as human beings in a direct encounter of mutual encouragement, acceptance, understanding, and love. At such times, it is not Filipinoness or Americanness but humanness that matters.

It was a magnificent adventure, and to the query, "Are you glad you were in it, knowing now, as you could not before, its physically and emotionally bruising and exhausting qualities?" I would answer with most Peace Corps volunteers, "You bet I am!"